# CRAFTS FOR KIDS
## A MONTH-BY-MONTH
## IDEA BOOK

To my wonderful husband, Dan, and to my children,
Terry, Barbara, Elizabeth, and Mary.

No. 1784
$17.95

# CRAFTS FOR KIDS
## A MONTH-BY-MONTH
## IDEA BOOK

### BY BARBARA L. DONDIEGO
### ILLUSTRATED BY JACQUELINE CAWLEY

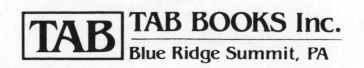

TAB BOOKS Inc.
Blue Ridge Summit, PA

FIRST EDITION

TENTH PRINTING

Printed in the United States of America

Library of Congress Cataloging in Publication Data

Dondiego, Barbara L.
Crafts for kids.

Includes index.
1. Handicraft.   I. Title.
TT157.D63   1984      745.5      84-16439
ISBN 0-8306-0784-6
ISBN 0-8306-1784-1 (pbk.)

TAB BOOKS Inc. offers software for
sale. For information and a catalog,
please contact TAB Software Department,
Blue Ridge Summit, PA 17294-0850.

Questions regarding the content of this book
should be addressed to:

Reader Inquiry Branch
TAB BOOKS Inc.
Blue Ridge Summit, PA 17294-0214

Cover photograph by the Ziegler
Photography Studio of Waynesboro, PA.

# Contents

# Introduction

The purpose of this book of crafts is to give parents and other interested adults a handbook of creative ways to teach young children. Children love seasonal crafts, and this book is full of them. Some of the projects can be done alone by the children, but most of the crafts are designed for adults who want imaginative ideas for creating with young people ages 2 through 10.

Craft-training, *the method used in this book,* prepares children to participate in school without taking the place of school. It teaches children preschool skills methodically and purposefully, while showing them how to create with craft materials that are inexpensive and easy to find. The children end each craft session with an interesting and often decorative product, and with a better understanding of the preschool skills emphasized by the craft. The crafts themselves are precisely written, with suggestions for what the adult can say to the child to teach particular skills. The realistic illustrations will help you to guide children to successful completed projects.

There are two big differences between this craft book and others on the market. First, these crafts are inexpensive. Most of them are made from things that can be found in the supermarket and drugstore. The school and office supplies section of these stores yields everything from scissors and glue to permanent markers. Pipe cleaners are found in the smoking section. Flour for paste and for flour-salt dough is probably already in your kitchen cupboard. In other words, you do not need to raid an expensive craft store to interest your children in crafts. Movable, paste-on eyes and flexible strip magnets are used for several of the crafts, but they are rarely needed and are used simply because the children can make a different type of craft with them. To purchase these items you must go to a craft store and ask for them by name. The eyes come in packets of eight or more, and the magnets come on a large roll which can be cut with scissors. You will have enough of each to make several craft items.

The second thing that makes this book unique

is that it is a handbook for Craft-training, a new idea for teaching children the skills they need to succeed in school.

While making a craft, the child cuts with scissors, colors and pastes neatly, and paints with a brush. He counts and is repeatedly exposed to shapes, letters, sizes, and colors. As he manipulates the craft materials, he develops eye-hand coordination, which is the ability to make his hands and fingers do the things that his eyes want them to do. This skill is very important when the child learns writing and math. Any adult who has tried to thread a needle can understand what eye-hand coordination is!

As the child talks about the craft with an adult, he develops precise language skills, also important to school success. As he assembles the craft with an adult's guidance, he learns to listen, to follow directions, and to think and act in sequence. He knows the joy of sitting still long enough to make something himself. Children display their creations with great pride because they make them with their own hands.

Children can begin Craft-training at an early age, as young as 2 years old. By the time they enter kindergarten, they will have mastered the skills they need to succeed in school.

Each craft is presented with a list of materials needed to make the craft, a list of skills that can be taught with the craft, and exact instructions showing you how to teach it. Keywords that should be said to the child are *underlined*. Words such as *orange triangle* and *three white circles* are repeated in the natural process of making the craft. Without memorizing or being formally taught, the child will learn the skills needed for school, and you will be his teacher.

The cooking projects were included in this book for a very special reason. A child who is very active and physical and is on the go every minute of the day, is a child who could benefit a great deal from Craft-training, since schools will expect him to behave in a controlled manner. They will expect him to have an adequate attention span, to listen without interrupting, and to follow simple directions in order. Yet he may take no interest whatsoever in working with crafts if it means that he must sit still, listen, and follow directions for a few minutes. The best way that I have found to get his attention is with cooking activities. He will always be interested in eating, especially if the food is particularly yummy. When he discovers that he must participate in the making of the food project in order to eat his portion, his attention and cooperation increase dramatically.

When working with food, of course, he is immediately rewarded for his effort. He gets to consume his craft. This positive experience will be useful after a few craft sessions. It won't be long before he will happily work on nonfood crafts as well. Instead of eating it, he will show it off. This carry-over is sometimes the only way that you will gain a child's cooperative effort, and you can always go back to using edible crafts if the child's interest wanes.

If you doubt the need for teaching a child before he or she enters kindergarten, consider the following true case histories.

Tony comes from a bilingual family that moved to this country 1 month before he was born. His relatives visit often, and the language of his parents' old country is spoken in the home. He entered school speaking poor English and knowing very little about school skills. His parents assumed the school would teach him whatever he needed to learn. He has just completed a year of kindergarten, and he has just failed his first year in school.

Linda is the youngest in a family of 4 children. Her oldest brother is 17 and has always done well in school. Her parents were eager for her to begin kindergarten because they felt that she was ready to learn. On the first day of school her kindergarten teacher used a yellow marker to highlight her name, plus the name of every other child entering school with her who had a birthday prior to December 1. She and her fellow age-mates were then grouped together for all lessons. Often, several times a week, her teacher "team-taught" with another kindergarten teacher. This meant that Linda was included in a group of nearly 60 5-year-olds for some classes. She has just completed her year of kindergarten, and she has just failed her first year in school.

John has two parents who work very hard at their jobs. They both must hold down good paying jobs to afford their home mortgage, their pool, the two cars, the boats, and the summer vacation cabin by a Michigan lake. They assumed that their son would learn whatever he needed to know when he started school. So for nine hours a day, five days a week since he was an infant, John was left in custodial day care. This is babysitting in which the children are fed and kept clean and safe, but are taught very little. When John entered kindergarten, he had trouble sitting still, listening, and learning. He failed his first year of kindergarten, even though the sociologist and psychologist who tested him say that he has above average intelligence and no learning disability that they can pinpoint. John is presently enrolled in a special education class. He will remain there until the school says that he is ready to be placed in a group of his peers. John is 8 years old. He has been a failure since age 5, and he knows it.

If the parents of these three children had been aware that their children had to be prepared for entering school, these stories could have been different. If these children had been taught school-related skills before entering kindergarten, they most likely would not have failed. It must be a terrible thing to fail when you're only 5 years old, and when kindergarten is the most important thing you've ever done in your life.

In 1973 it was common for children to enter school knowing nothing. I remember my first day as a first grade teacher that year. There were 2 boys named "Randall" assigned to my class of 27 students. They had arrived on the school bus without name tags or parents, of course, so I had no way of knowing which Randall was which. I decided to ask.

"Randall," I said, pulling the 6-year-old closer to me, "Which one are you? Randall Fitzgerald or Randall Cline?" Randall looked completely blank.

"I don't know," he said after a long pause. "I'll tell you tomorrow." Randall had started first grade at age 6 without even knowing his last name.

I thought the incident was pretty funny, but it really was not that unusual. Children were expected to learn at school. They were not expected to know anything before that time, except how to go to the bathroom alone.

In 1973 children who failed to learn the skills taught them during the school year were either passed onto the next grade where it was hoped they would learn the next year with a little more maturity under their belts, or they repeated the grade. The ones held back, however, were few and far between. They consisted mainly of children who were really struggling to learn and just could not keep up.

In less than 10 years that situation changed dramatically. Suddenly the preschool child who enters kindergarten before his fifth birthday must know many, many things without being formally taught. He certainly must know his last name, and he should be aware of his mother's and father's names, his complete address, his telephone number, and his birthdate, because he will be expected to memorize these things within the first two weeks of kindergarten.

Before a child sets foot inside the kindergarten door, he or she must know:

- How to hold a pencil properly for writing
- How to color "within the lines" using realistic colors. For example, if he colors blue hair, that may be creative, but it is not realistic. Scribbling is also unacceptable
- How to read his first and last name
- How to print his first name, using capital and lowercase letters
- How to recognize numbers up to 10
- How to count out loud up to 20
- How to follow directions given by an adult
- How to think and act in sequence, such as "First we do this. Next we do this"
- How to cut neatly with scissors
- How to paste and glue neatly, without eating the paste
- How to draw a recognizable person
- How to paint with a brush without mixing up

all the colors

- The names of the five basic shapes: square, circle, triangle, rectangle, and diamond
- The names of all basic colors: red, yellow, blue, orange, green, purple, black, white, brown, and pink

If a child begins kindergarten without knowing these things he will be behind on the first day of school. Be assured that there are parents who will make sure that their children learn these skills before starting school. All other children must compete with them. Children should also know how to button, snap, zip, and tie a bow because this will give them an air of independence that will impress their teacher.

The schools are ready to teach phonics (the sound each letter makes in a word), how to read color words, how to write to 20 and beyond, how many make a dozen. They will teach him to read number and color words, to count to 100, and to count by fives and tens. They will teach him to spell and print his last name and to measure with a ruler, but they have very little patience with a child who is overwhelmed by the amount of mental growth expected of him in that first short year.

If the child is 5 years, 3 months, or younger, on the day he enters school, if he comes from a bilingual home, if his parents read very little and perhaps use improper English, if both parents work and he is given custodial care for the first 4 years of his life, if he is allowed simply to grow up without being taught, he will probably be unable to keep up with the amount of material expected of him.

Today children who show the slightest weakness in kindergarten are labeled by the school system. They are given mental tests whose validity is suspect. Then they are grouped in special education classes instead of regular first grade. On the surface this appears to be an excellent solution. Supposedly the child is not stigmatized by having to repeat kindergarten. Supposedly he is taught a concentrated amount of kindergarten first grade type material, and allowed to mature for a year, and then is "main-streamed" into a regular first grade class the following year. In actuality he is held back from his peer group. The test records are part of his permanent file, which means they follow him forever. The child knows, and his peers know, that he has failed kindergarten—a failure at age five.

The main problem does not lie with the child. He will learn if he is taught. The problem lies with the school and with parents. No one told the mother whose first child is now in grade seven, and whose youngest child is now entering kindergarten that things have changed in the school system. Much more is expected of the preschooler, but the parents of that preschooler are being caught off guard and unprepared. They still count on the school to completely educate their children. The sad part is that schools do not consider it their responsibility to teach children the basics that they are supposed to know. If the child comes to school unprepared, the school points the finger at his parents.

"Why didn't they teach him?" the teacher asks.

"Why didn't someone tell the parents how and what to teach him?" I ask.

Because of the need to teach my own children at a very early age at home, I began Craft-training. Any parent knows that a 2-year-old child will balk at being made to sit down and write his numbers and letters and memorize his colors. Flash cards have their place in teaching a preschooler, but basically they are boring. They are useful only when the child wants to use them.

"My child will not let me teach him," is a complaint that I hear often from parents. "He's not interested in learning. He won't sit still long enough. He doesn't like to say his alphabet."

With Craft-training, children will learn the basic skills needed for school success, but they will not realize they are being taught. By following the directions outlined in each project, any adult can be a teacher. It's fun; it's easy, and it will give your child a head start in learning school skills.

# 1: January Crafts

Children can make the projects for January at the kitchen table while you keep an eye on supper. Except for watercolor painting, which can drag on for an hour or so, each craft takes only a few minutes of your time and very little of your money.

## EYE-HAND COORDINATION AND SMALL MOTOR SKILLS

The list of skills the children will learn by making these crafts involves basic abilities. They are skills that everyone should learn as early as possible. During every craft, the children make their eyes, hands, and fingers work together. These skills are called "eye-hand coordination" and "small motor skills." At school, when a child must follow words with his eyes to learn reading and writing, or must copy letters and figures onto a paper, these abilities are very important. If you help him practice eye-hand coordination and small motor skills at as young an age as possible, he will grow amazingly adept at them.

"Large motor skills," incidentally, are being practiced when the children climb, run, jump down the stairs, fall over furniture on purpose, slide down the railing, leap through the hallway, and generally drive you crazy by being in the house all winter.

The next time your child is acting in such a manner, and you want to sound particularly knowledgeable, just scream, "Jimmy, will you please stop practicing your large motor skills!" It may not be a very effective way to calm him down, but at least you will give the impression of being in control of the situation.

## CRAFT-TRAINING SKILLS TO LEARN

The crafts in this chapter do not have to be done in any order. Select one that interests you and your child, check the Materials List to see if you have the necessary items on hand, and approach it with the idea that you are going to use that craft to teach your child the school-related skills that are listed with it.

Craft-training skills to practice in January include:

• Learning the names of colors

- How to glue
- How to read his or her name
- How to print his or her name. (The printing will start out looking very strange, but will get better as the child gets older.)
- How to use paints
- How to draw a face
- Learning the basic geometric shapes
- Counting to 10
- Learning the meaning of *under, on top of, inside,* and *a pair*
- Learning to use descriptive words
- How to cut. ("Practice makes perfect," you know; so don't be afraid to give your 2-year-old rounded safety scissors. Just don't let him cut his hair, or his brother's.)

## BALLOON MAN

When the children are getting restless cooped up inside on dreary January days, let Balloon Man come to your rescue (Fig. 1-1). He will provide safe indoor play as the children use their muscle power to throw him around. No matter how he is tossed about, however, he always lands on his feet.

### Skills to Teach

Teach children 2 years old and up:

- The color of the balloon
- How to read his or her name
- How to draw a face

Teach children 5 years old and up:

- How to blow up and tie a balloon
- How to cut out feet

### Materials List

- A 9-inch balloon for each Balloon Man
- Construction paper or lightweight cardboard
- Scissors
- Permanent markers
- Transparent tape

### Directions

Let everyone choose a balloon. Emphasize the balloon's color. Say, "What color balloon do you want, Mary?" Mary does not know her colors; so she does not say anything. She points to a balloon. "Do you want a *red* one? Here is a *round, red* balloon for you." Give Mary the balloon.

Blow up the balloon for everyone who cannot do it. Tie the end in a fat knot.

Cut out a foot for each Balloon Man by tracing the pattern in Fig. 1-2. Children 5 years old and up can cut their own if you draw it for them. Have them draw toes or shoelaces on the foot.

Insert the balloon's knot in Cut A of the foot, so that the knot is on the bottom. A small piece of tape will hold the cut shut so the knot will not pop out.

Each child, using permanent markers, should draw a face on his or her own balloon. Closely supervise the children when they use permanent markers, because the markers stain.

Print the child's name on the back of the Balloon Man's head. Use both uppercase and lowercase letters. The children will read their own names and find their own particular balloon's color each time they throw the balloons around.

## POPCORN SNOWMAN

January and snowmen go together naturally, even if you live where there is never any snow. Of course a 2- or 3-year-old cannot cut out a very good circle; so you must cut the shapes before the activity begins. When young children put together precut shapes, they practice eye-hand coordination, and they have an attractive craft to call their own (Fig 1-3).

### Skills to Teach

Teach children 2 years old and up:

- The colors *white, red, black,* and *orange*
- The *circle, triangle, square,* and *rectangle* shapes
- How many make *3*

Teach children 4 years old and up cutting skills.

### Materials List

- Popcorn for popping
- White construction paper or typing paper

Fig. 1-1. The Balloon Man.

Fig. 1-2. The feet for Balloon Man.

- Black and orange construction paper
- Nontoxic white glue
- Jar lids to put glue in
- Scissors
- Table salt (optional)
- Extra construction paper, any color

Fig. 1-3. The Popcorn Snowman.

## Directions

Pop the corn, using as little oil as possible. A hot air popper is ideal because oil will seep out into the construction paper if you use too much. Put it, unsalted, in a big bowl so everyone can reach it.

Draw three circles of graduated sizes on white paper for each snowman; you can use the patterns in Figs 1-4 and 1-5. If you plan to make several Popcorn Snowmen, stack the white papers together and cut several shapes at one time.

Using the patterns, trace the square "top of hat," the rectangle "brim of hat," and two circle eyes onto black paper. Trace the triangle nose onto orange paper, and the mouth onto red paper.

Children 4 years old and up can cut their own shapes. Cut them out for younger children before the craft session begins. Don't expect the children to sit and watch you cut out shapes for 10 minutes. They will eat all the popcorn and then run off to play.

Pour a small amount of white glue into a jar lid for each child. Be sure to use nontoxic glue in case the children decide to have a snack while making this craft.

Give each child all the shapes he will need to make the snowman. Then tell the children the following: "Glue the *three white circles* onto the piece of construction paper so that they make a snowman. Use the *large circle* for the snowman's bottom, the *middle-sized circle* for the snowman's middle, and the *small circle* for the head." Help each child to do it correctly so the snowman is not laying down sideways or standing on his head.

Tell them to put the *black rectangle* about 1/3 of the way down the snowman's head for a hat brim. Then they can glue the *black square above* the brim to complete the hat.

Show the children how to dip each piece of popcorn in the glue and stick it on the circles. They can continue to do this step until the snowman is covered or until they get tired. No matter how they do it, the craft will look pretty good.

Tell the children to glue on the *two black circle* eyes, the *orange triangle* nose, and the *red* mouth.

A background can be added with crayons. If you want to get really fancy, brush white glue on the background and cover it with table salt. Shake off the excess and let it dry for a sparkly effect.

When you display the Popcorn Snowman, tape it up high, or the children will try to eat it later.

---

### NOTE

Count everything out loud. After awhile it will become such a habit that you will find yourself counting even when no child is around!

*Count stairs as you go up or down.*
*How many kisses to erase a frown.*
*Count buttons as you fasten his jacket.*
*How many shushes to quiet their racket.*
("That's ONE!")
*Count bites of peas upon her plate.*
*Before you know it, they'll be counting great!*

---

## PAPER STRIP SNOWMAN

This Paper Strip Snowman will stand by himself as a winter centerpiece (Fig. 1-6).

### Skills to Teach

Teach children 2 years old and up:

• The colors *white, black, red,* and *yellow*
• The *rectangle* and *circle* shapes
• How many make *3*

Teach children 4 years old and up cutting and gluing skills.

### Materials List

• White, black, red, and yellow construction paper
• Ruler and pencil
• Scissors
• Glue
• A stapler (optional)

### Directions

Using a pencil and ruler, divide a sheet of white construction paper into three rectangles for each snowman. Make the first rectangle 2 × 6 inches. Make the second rectangle 3 × 8 inches. Make the third rectangle 4 × 12 inches.

On the colored construction paper, draw black,

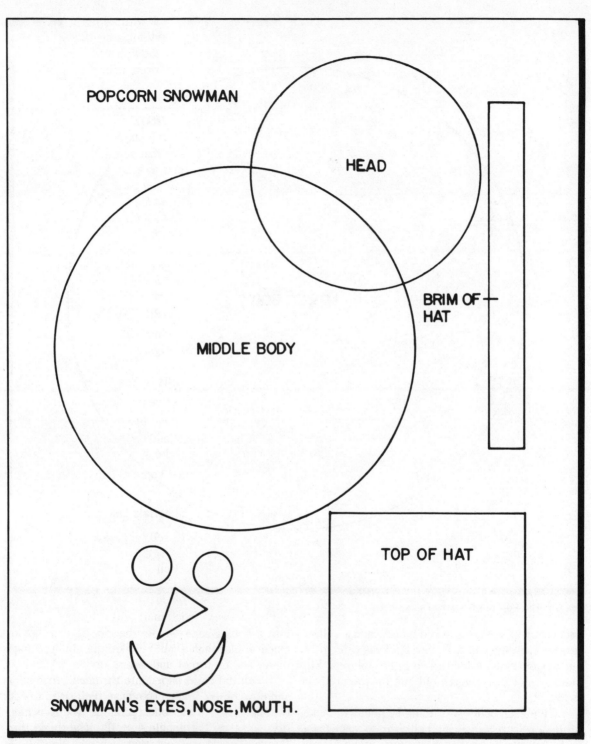

POPCORN SNOWMAN

HEAD

BRIM OF HAT

MIDDLE BODY

TOP OF HAT

SNOWMAN'S EYES, NOSE, MOUTH.

Fig. 1-4. The patterns to make the Popcorn Snowman.

Fig. 1-5. The Popcorn Snowman's lower body.

circular eyes and nose, a red mouth, and a yellow pipe for each snowman. Draw a black hat (Fig. 1-7). Cut out everything for the younger children. Encourage children 4 years old and up to cut their own.

Give each child everything he needs to make the Paper Strip Snowman. Tell them to make *three circles* by overlapping each *rectangle* and gluing it into a *circle* shape. Staple the circles together to make a snowman shape, or let the children glue them, one on top of the other.

Tell the children to glue the *black circle* eyes and nose on the snowman's face. Tell them to add the *black* hat and the *yellow* pipe. Let the snowmen dry, and then flatten the bottoms slightly so that they will stand up.

Fig. 1-6. The Paper Strip Snowman.

Fig. 1-7. The patterns to make the Paper Strip Snowman.

## WATERCOLOR PAINTING

Painting with watercolors is a lot of fun for children and needn't be hard on you. I know many mothers who will not buy their children paints, markers, scissors, and glue because they can't stand messes. This doesn't have to be the case, however. Just pull up long sleeves and put a paint smock on everyone; a large shirt turned backwards works fine.

### Skills to Teach

Teach children 2 years old and up:

- The names of colors
- How to read his or her name
- How to paint without mixing up the colors

### Materials List

- Old newspapers to cover the kitchen table
- A watercolor paint set and a brush for each child
- Cups or bowls for rinse water. (Choose ones that do not tip easily.)
- White paper. (I use discarded computer paper. If you know anyone who is a secretary, see if you can get discarded typing paper, or buy plain white paper.)

## Directions

Lay down several thicknesses of newspaper on your kitchen table. Lay down some ground rules for the children, too, such as: "Paint the paper only. If you paint yourself, your neighbor, or the walls you will lose your right to paint forevermore. Do not bring your drippy painting to show me when I am in the bedroom trying to change the sheets. Leave the painting flat in front of you and wait for me to discover it. Do not get out of your seat and change your own rinse water. In fact, do not get out of your seat at all until I can help you." With these simple rules everyone can enjoy being an artist.

Show the children how to rub a wet brush on the paint and transfer the color to their paper. Show them how to rinse their brushes so that the colors do not mix together.

Comment on their paintings by saying, "What a nice *red* (or whatever color they are using) design," or "I like your painting. I see that you're using *purple* and *black*."

You can also emphasize painting skills and colors by saying to a particular child, "Terry, let's use *yellow* this time." Hold Terry's hand and help him swish his brush in the yellow paint. Then let him paint his paper with this brush full of yellow.

If a child can sit in a high chair, he can paint. Put a bib on the child and tape a piece of painting paper to the high chair tray. Fasten a set of watercolors to the tray by rolling up two or three pieces of tape and sticking them on the bottom of the paint set. Add a little bit of water to all the colors—a pump sprayer, such as an old hair spray or window cleaner bottle filled with water, is handy for this. Give him a brush and show him how to dip into the paints. Take away his painting as soon as he is finished, and let him get down as soon as he is bored. Do not give him rinse water unless you plan to mop the floor that day.

One word of caution: adults feel most comfortable when children paint things that we can recognize. Children just like to paint. Try not to say, "What is it?" when you look at their creations.

Snowy day pictures look really special if glitter is added to the picture. Brush on white glue and pour on glitter. Shake the excess glitter onto waxed paper and return it to the glitter bottle. Glitter can often be found in the drugstore if no craft store is handy. Even a 2-year-old's smudges can be titled "A Snowy Day" if glitter is added.

---

### NOTE

White chalk shows up great on black paper. The children can draw snowmen, snowy scenes, or falling snow. Spray with artist's fixative, which you can find in a craft store, or with hairspray so the chalk will not rub off easily.

---

## FISH BOWL

The Fish Bowl is a delight for children to both make and display (Fig. 1-8). The rice and shells give it a three-dimensional effect.

### Skills to Teach

Teach children 2 years old and up:

- The colors *blue, orange,* and *white*
- The meaning of *on top of*
- To count to *10*
- Gluing skills
- How to print his or her name

Teach children 4 years old and up cutting skills.

### Materials List

- Blue and white construction paper
- Orange construction paper
- Rice
- Small shell macaroni
- Scissors
- Glue

### Directions

For each child, use the pattern in Fig. 1-9 to trace the fish bowl in the middle of the white paper. Carefully cut it out. Children 4 years old and up should cut their own. Keep the paper outline of the bowl and discard the cutout.

Trace on orange paper and cut out a set of ten fish for each child. Let the older children cut their own. As you give each child his set of *ten orange* fish, count the fish together, out loud.

Tell the children to glue the *white* paper that has the fish bowl outline, *on top of* the *blue* paper so the edges of the papers are even. This "fills" the fish bowl with *blue* "water."

Tell the children to glue grains of rice on the bottom of the fish bowl to make "sand" by squirting glue on the picture, piling rice on the glue, and shaking off the excess. Then they can add "sea shells" by gluing on shell macaroni.

Tell the children to glue their *ten orange* fish in the bowl, counting out loud as they glue.

---

**NOTE**

Turtles and frogs spend January hibernating in the mud or under warm leaves. This is a good time of year for a nature lesson, even if you can't go outside. Visit your library with the children and find books about animals in winter. Read or tell the children stories about the animals.

---

Make sure each child prints his or her name on the finished picture so that everyone can tell who made it. Hold his hand lightly if necessary so that he holds the pencil correctly and writes the uppercase and lowercase letters neatly.

## FROG

This Frog is a project the children can keep as a toy, after they've made it (Fig. 1-10).

### Skills to Teach

Teach children 2 years old and up:

- The colors *red* and *green*
- How many legs a frog has
- How many make *2* and how many make *4*
- The *square* shape
- Gluing skills

Teach children 4 years old and up cutting skills

### Materials List

The first four items must be purchased in a craft or fabric store.

Fig. 1-8. The Fishbowl.

Fig. 1-9. The patterns for the Fishbowl and Fish.

Fig. 1-10. The Frog.

- 3″ styrofoam balls
- Green felt material
- Red felt material
- 2 movable paste-on eyes, size 10 MM, for each frog
- Green tissue wrapping paper.(Look in the card section of grocery and drug stores.)
- Scissors
- Glue

### Directions

Cut the styrofoam balls in half with a sharp knife. Each ball makes two frogs.

Cut the green tissue into a 6-×-6-inch square for each frog.

For each child, trace the frog's four feet onto the green felt. Trace his tongue onto the red felt. Children 4 years old and up can cut out their own felt and tissue shapes, if you draw them first, and if they have scissors that are sharp enough (Fig. 1-11).

Give each child 1/2 of a styrofoam ball, one square of green tissue paper, four legs, two eyes, and a tongue.

Tell them to wrap the *green* tissue paper *square*

around their styrofoam ball so that the rounded top is smooth. They should overlap the edges of the tissue paper underneath the flat side of the ball and glue them in place. This step can get a little messy, so be ready with a wet cloth for sticky fingers.

Next, tell the children to glue the *four green* legs underneath the frog's body so that they stick out in the right places.

Tell the children to glue the frog's *red* tongue underneath his body so that it sticks out where his face will be.

Glue on *two* eyes, spaced far apart.

### PAPER PLATE FROG

The very cheapest white generic paper plates make wonderful material for art work, such as this Paper Plate Frog (Fig. 1-12). They do not have a design to interfere with your craft and they are not heavily waxed, which makes it easy to color on them with crayons and markers. Just don't serve macaroni and cheese on them.

### Skills to Teach

Teach children 2 years old and up:

- The colors *white* and *green*
- How many make *2* and how many make *4*
- How to print his or her name

Teach children 4 years old and up:

- Cutting and gluing skills
- The meaning of *under, on top of,* and *inside*

### Materials List

- A plain white paper plate for each child
- Green construction paper
- Crayons
- Scissors
- Glue

### Directions

Help each child fold a *white* paper plate in half to make the frog's body and mouth combined.

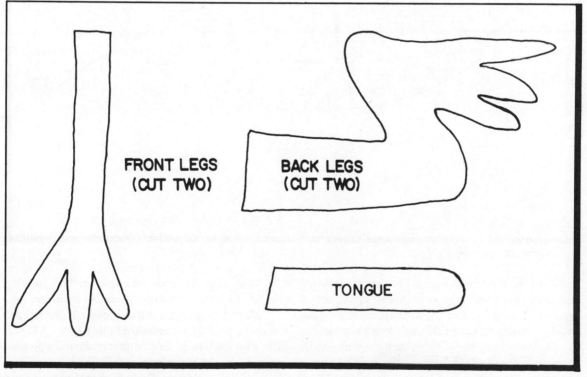

FRONT LEGS
(CUT TWO)

BACK LEGS
(CUT TWO)

TONGUE

Fig. 1-11. The patterns to make the Frog.

Fig. 1-12. The Paper Plate Frog.

Use the pattern in Fig. 1-13 to trace two back legs and two front legs onto green construction paper for each frog. Cut these shapes out for your smaller child; encourage children 4 years old and up to cut their own. Have tape handy for mending, because it's hard for children to cut skinny frog arms and toes.

Trace two eyes onto green paper. The children can cut them out and draw eyeballs on them.

Make a long tongue so the frog can catch flies. Cut a strip of green construction paper 1/4 × 8 inches for each frog. Curl it tightly around a pencil, and remove the pencil.

Tell the children to glue *four green* legs *under*

the frog's body. Tell them to glue the *two green* eyes *on top of* the frog's head so that they stick up. Tell them to glue the *green* curled tongue *inside* the frog's mouth.

The children can color the frogs with *green* crayons. They can color the inside of the mouth red or green and can draw *two* dots for his nose.

Each person should print his or her name on the bottom of his frog. Make sure the children hold their crayons correctly for coloring or writing, and that they use uppercase and lowercase letters in their name.

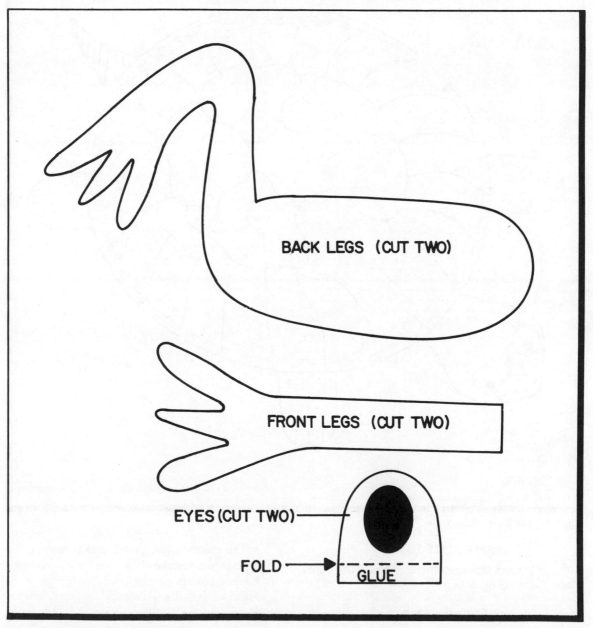

Fig. 1-13. The patterns to make the Paper Plate Frog.

Fig. 1-14. The Paper Plate Turtle.

### PAPER PLATE TURTLE

Another project that uses paper plates is the Paper Plate Turtle (Fig. 1-14).

### Skills to Teach

Teach children 2 years old and up:

- The colors *white, green,* and *brown*
- How many make *4*
- Gluing skills
- Coloring skills

Teach children 4 years old and up cutting skills.

## Materials List

- 9-inch paper plates
- Green construction paper
- Green and brown crayons
- Scissors
- Glue

## Directions

For each turtle, trace and cut out four feet, a pointed tail, and a head from green paper (Fig. 1-15). Children 4 years old and up can cut out their own if you draw them first.

Show the children how to decorate the *bottom* of the paper plate to resemble a turtle shell, using *green* and *brown* crayons. You might want to draw the shell design on the plate for younger children, and let them color it.

Tell the children to glue the *four green* feet to the underside of the turtle's shell. Tell them to glue the *green* head and *green* tail to the underside, also.

As soon as his turtle dries, each child can draw eyes, nose holes, and a mouth on the turtle's head with crayons. Then he can turn the turtle over and print his name on the underside of the shell. Help the children hold their crayons correctly when coloring and writing.

## CRISPY RICE SNOWBALLS

Remind the children that these Crispy Rice Snowballs are the only snowballs that are safe to eat, since the real ones outside have a high lead content caused by air pollution (Fig. 1-16).

## Skills to Teach

Teach children 2 years old and up:

- To sit still, listen, and follow directions
- To count to *9*
- How to read his or her name
- To use words such as *sticky, crisp, firmly,* and *delicious*

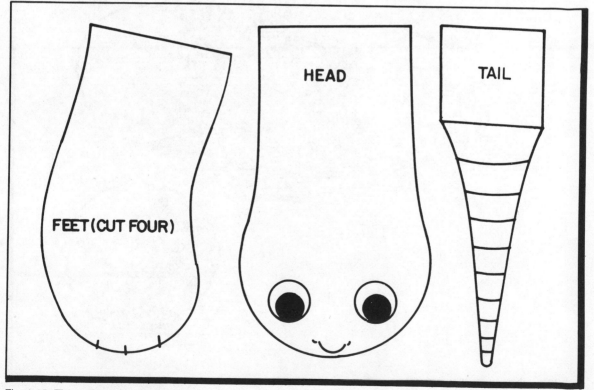

Fig. 1-15. The patterns for the Paper Plate Turtle.

## Materials List

- 1/2 cup margarine (1 stick)
- 16 ounces marshmallows (1 pound)
- 9 cups crisp rice cereal (Generic cereal works very well.)
- A paper plate for each child
- Cinnamon redhots (Optional)
- A large bowl and a wooden spoon

## Directions

Melt the margarine and marshmallows in the top of a double boiler. Remove from the heat.

*Microwave Directions:* combine the margarine and marshmallows in a microwave bowl. Cover with plastic wrap. Microwave on *high* for 3 minutes. Remove from the oven.

Stir with a wooden spoon until smooth. Do this step on a table where the children can see. Show them how *sticky* the mixture is.

Help the children add *9* cups of crisp rice cereal. Count out loud with the children as they add the cups of cereal, "One . . . two . . . three . . . four . . . five . . . six . . . seven . . . eight . . . nine. How many cups of cereal did we add? *Nine.*"

The children can take turns stirring this mixture with a wooden spoon. Have them do it one at a time, though, or you will have cereal all over the kitchen.

Fig. 1-16. Crispy Rice Snowballs.

Fig. 1-17. Peanut Butter/Apple Slices.

Print each child's name on his or her paper plate, using uppercase and lowercase letters.

Spoon a large portion onto each child's plate. Give everyone 1/2 teaspoon of margarine to rub on the palms of their hands.

Tell the children to shape their portion into a snowball, pressing it *firmly* together. Refrigerate the snowballs on the plates until they become firm, about 30 minutes. The children can make faces on their snowballs with cinnamon redhots before they are refrigerated, if you wish.

Help the children pick out their own snowball by reading the name on the plate. Note how *delicious* the snowballs taste by asking, "Aren't these *delicious* and *crisp*?"

## PEANUT BUTTER/APPLE SLICES

A good time to teach children small tidbits of information is when they're sitting at the table eating tidbits of food. They are a captive audience for sure. With this snack they will learn about apples and pairs (Fig. 1-17).

### Skills to Teach

Teach children 2 years old and up:

- The meaning of *a pair*
- How many make *2*
- How to spread with a knife
- How to read his or her name

### Materials List

- Paper plates
- 1 apple for each child
- Peanut butter
- A table knife or a plastic picnic knife for each child

### Directions

Print each child's name, using uppercase and lowercase letters, on his paper plate.

Slice and core an apple for each child. Peel them if needed. I know the peeling is good for you, but my children spit it out, and I would rather peel the apples than clean up spit-out peelings.

Give each child as many apple slices as you think he will eat and a lump of peanut butter on a paper plate.

Tell the children to spread peanut butter on one apple slice, stick on another apple slice, and eat the whole thing. Say to them, "We use *2* apple slices to make each snack. We use a *pair* of apple slices for each snack. How many make a *pair? Two!*"

As soon as they understand that, let them spread and eat in peace.

# 2: February Crafts

Do your children know who chopped his father's cherry tree? Do they know why Lincoln Logs have that name? February offers a chance to teach a few facts about American History, and Valentine's Day is a wonderful way to brighten up a cold, dark, winter month.

### CRAFT-TRAINING SKILLS TO LEARN

Trying a new craft is like trying a new recipe. Just assemble the ingredients, put your imagination into gear, and follow the directions. Add a touch of this or that as you wish, to make the finished product your very own.

Use February crafts to teach the following skills:

- Learning the names of colors
- How to glue
- How to print his name
- How to draw a face
- Learning the basic geometric shapes
- Counting
- Learning *how many* make 2, 3, and 4

- How to cut, sew, and string a necklace, which teach eye-hand coordination and small motor skills.
- Learning to use descriptive words
- Learning the meaning of *large* and *small, top* and *bottom, between,* and *cooporation*
- Learning to sit still, listen, and follow directions with cooking crafts

### CHILDREN LEARN AS THEY COOK

A child needs to know what goes into a recipe, just as he needs to know that green beans and milk come from a farm and not just a grocery store.

I know a man who loved to eat pudding until he discovered that it was made with eggs and milk. Now he hates it. I taught a class of first graders who wouldn't taste the cookie dough I brought them because they thought it was clay. "Oh no," they all said in unison, "We're not gonna taste that stuff! You can't trick us!" Only Wanda Jean would taste the dough because her mother baked cookies, and she knew what it was. I know another man who recently found out that pickles are made from cucumbers, raisins come from dried grapes, and prunes are dried-up plums.

It reminds me of a Chicago columnist who was realizing some facts of country life. When he was a child he could never figure out what a veal was. His mother bought it at the grocers and he ate it, but he had never seen one. Finally he imagined a veal to be a four-legged creature that walked around in the country. His favorite Italian dish was fettuccine. He decided that when he grew up he wanted to move to the country and grow a garden full of fettuccine, but then, he thought, that wouldn't work because the veals would probably eat it.

Cook with your children. It teaches them a lot of things.

## PRETZEL LOG CABIN

Abraham Lincoln was born February 12, 1809, in Hodgenville, Kentucky. His birthplace was a small 16-×-18-foot log cabin with one window and a dirt floor. He was the 16th president of the United States.

To understand how a log cabin looked nearly 200 years ago, you can help the children build one from Lincoln Logs, or the children can make a much cheaper model from fat pretzel sticks (Fig. 2-1). I prefer the pretzel stick log cabin because after the house-raising the children can pretend to be termites and eat the house.

It was necessary for people to cooperate 200 years ago, working together to build houses and barns. Since the main tools available were hatchets, saws, and hammers, everyone had to pitch in and help his neighbor build the log cabin structures that made up the pioneer farm. The children's pretzel log cabin teaches them about cooperation as they take turns helping with the house-raising.

Fig. 2-1. The Pretzel Log Cabin.

## Skills to Teach

Teach children 2 years old and up:

- The *square* shape
- The colors *brown* and *green*
- The meaning of *cooperate*

Teach children 3 years old and up:

- Some historic facts about our country
- To use descriptive words such as *salty*, *crisp*, and *crunchy*

## Materials List

- A 9-ounce bag of pretzel rods. (Fat pretzels about 7″ long, found in the snack section of supermarkets.)
  - A sheet of green construction paper
  - A sheet of brown construction paper

## Directions

Tell the children who Abraham Lincoln was, and why we celebrate his birthday. Visit the public library and look for books on our American ancestors, the pioneers. Talk about the log cabins that were the houses for many pioneers.

Tell them, "We're going to make a *square* log cabin, and we will use pretzels instead of logs. We need to *cooperate* and work together to build our square log cabin, just as the pioneers did."

Divide the pretzels as evenly as possible among the children. Lay the sheet of green construction paper on the table. Tell the children that the *green* paper can be the *green* grass where they will build their cabin.

Help the children work together, laying the pretzels in a crisscross fashion to form a square cabin. Point out that the cabin is a *square* since each side is the same length. Help the children understand the idea of *cooperation*—that they are building the cabin by taking turns and working together.

When the cabin is complete, say to the children, "Now I will fold this sheet of *brown* paper in half to make a roof for the cabin." Lay the roof carefully atop of the cabin.

Before the children dismantle their creation for snack time, talk about it a little more. Note the spaces, or *chinks*, between the logs and ask the children if they know how President Lincoln's family kept the cold wind out of their house. (They filled the chinks with clay from a river bank, mixed with straw or dried grass. They also covered their windows with oiled paper that let the light in, and used shutters when they wanted to close the windows tightly.)

As the children eat their pretzels, ask them to think of words that describe the pretzels. Print the words in large letters on a sheet of paper as they say them, then read the words back to the children. Some descriptive words you can encourage them to use are *salty*, *hard*, *crunchy*, *crisp*, and *crumbly*. Tape their list of descriptive words down low where they can look at it whenever they want.

Abraham Lincoln read books by candlelight and firelight in the evenings. Try reading a story to the children by candlelight. The effect is interesting. Stick a short candle inside a tall glass to make it safer.

---

### *NOTE*

When children are small, the *process* of creating is more important to them than the *product*. That is why they will work on something for a long time, and when it is finished will show very little interest in it!

---

## TRAY EMBROIDERY

Tray Embroidery is a *process* craft that children can do as long as they want. It's easy to do when the child uses a styrofoam meat tray, a large plastic needle, and yarn. Older children can create lovely and interesting designs using many different colors of yarn. Younger children will sew just for the sake of sewing (Fig. 2-2).

## Skills to Teach

Teach children 2 years old and up how-to sew. This is a very good activity to increase eye-hand coordination and small motor skills.

## Materials List

- Styrofoam meat trays

Fig. 2-2. Tray Embroidery.

• Yarn 18″ long

• Large plastic needles. (Look in the sewing and knitting notions section of your supermarket.)

### Directions

Wash and dry the meat trays.

*Tie* the yarn onto each needle, and tie a big knot at the other end of the yarn.

Show the children how to sew by poking the needle through a tray and turning the tray over and back. Don't expect them to do a perfect job, however. Let them do their own creating with this craft.

When they have finished sewing with the first piece of yarn, untie the needle, tie another piece of yarn to the first piece, and tie the needle on again. They can continue sewing for a long time this way.

### POM-POM CRITTER REFRIGERATOR MAGNET

The Pom-pom Critter Magnet is a good *product*

craft since the process of making it takes only a few minutes, and the child has a nice product to show off, play with, and keep. It's an excellent craft for little ones with short attention spans (Fig. 2-3).

### Skills to Teach

Teach children 2 years old and up:

• The colors *red* and *white*
• Gluing skills

Teach children 4 years old and up cutting skills.

### Materials List

The first 3 items must be purchased in a craft store. Just ask for them by name.

• 1 1/2″ white pom-poms
• Movable paste-on eyes, size 10 MM, 2 for each child

- 1/2″ wide flexible strip magnet, cut into 1″ pieces
- Red construction paper

### Directions

Use the pattern in Fig. 2-3 to trace a valentine foot onto red paper. Cut out one foot for each Critter. Children 4 years old and up should be encouraged to cut their own.

Give each child a pom-pom, two eyes, and a valentine foot. Tell them to put a small amount of glue in the middle of the *red* valentine, place the *white* pom-pom on the glue, and press down with their hand to stick the two together.

The children can glue on the eyes. Then they can add a 1-inch piece of magnet to the bottom of the Critter. The magnet comes with its own sticky backing and needs no glue.

After the Pom-Pom Critters dry, they can be used to decorate the refrigerator or to hold up notes or drawings.

## VALENTINE DOG

Another way to celebrate Valentine's Day is with a Valentine Dog. The children can make the dog from simple materials, with your help (Fig. 2-4).

### Skills to Teach

Teach children 2 years old and up:

- The color *red*
- How to draw a face
- Gluing skills
- To count to *4*
- How many make *2* and how many make *3*

Teach children 4 years old and up:

- To follow directions
- Cutting skills

### Materials List

- 3 pipe cleaners for each dog
- A 2″×3″ strip of red construction paper for each dog

FOOT

Fig. 2-3. The Pom-Pom Critter Refrigerator Magnet and pattern for his foot.

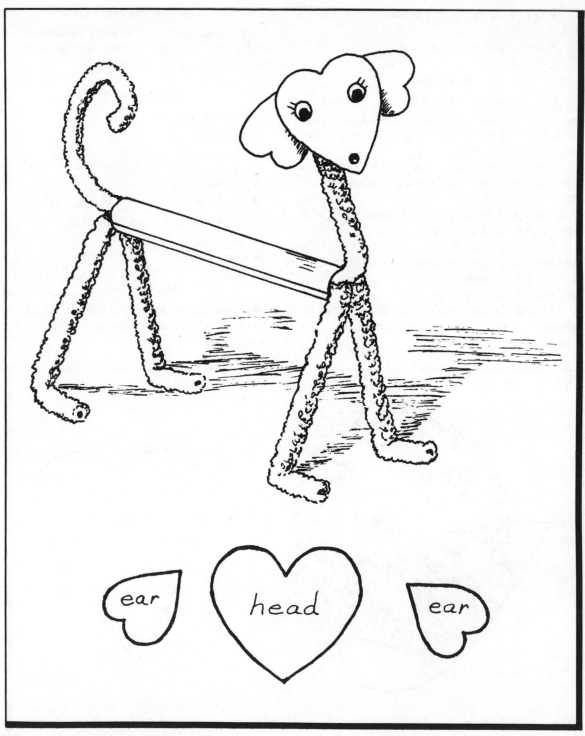

Fig. 2-4. The Valentine Dog and patterns.

- Red construction paper
- Scissors
- Glue

### Directions

For each child, use the pattern in Fig. 2-4 to trace the dog's head and ears onto the red paper. Cut them out for younger children, but encourage children 4 years old and up to cut their own.

As you hand three pipe cleaners to each child, say, "Please count these to see how many you have." To make sure they are not being cheated, the children will dutifully count them.

Give each child a valentine head, two ears, and a 2-×-3-inch red strip. Instruct the children by saying, "Hold the three pipe cleaners together so that the ends are even. Roll the strip of *red* paper tightly around the middle of the pipe cleaners. Glue the paper closed.

"Bend one pipe cleaner up at both ends for the dog's head and tail. Curl the tail. Make a 3/4-inch bend in the pipe cleaner that is the dog's head." You will have to help with this step.

"Bend the other two pipe cleaners down at both ends to form the front and back legs. Bend the tips of the pipe cleaners forward to form feet.

"Draw two eyes and a nose on the big *red* valentine.

"Glue the *red* valentine face onto the bent pipe cleaner at the dog's head. Glue the two *red* valentine ears onto the face." To your younger children you can add, "Your dog is done. You can play with him as soon as he dries. How many legs does he have? Let's count them." Count the legs out loud together.

The children can add a collar and leash from paper and string, if they wish.

### VALENTINE COOKIES

Roll-out cookies are easy and fun. All you need is a smooth plastic cloth on your kitchen table, a valentine cookie cutter, a rolling pin with a stockinette cover, and an apron. The rolling pin cover can be found in supermarkets, hardware stores, and kitchen speciality shops; it keeps the dough from sticking to the rolling pin.

### Skills to Teach

Teach children 2 years old and up:

- How to roll and cut cookie dough, which is much like clay
- To sit still, listen, and follow directions
- How to print his or her name

### Materials List

- A large bowl
- A wooden spoon or an electric mixer
- 3/4 cup shortening
- 1 cup sugar
- 2 eggs
- 1/2 teaspoon vanilla
- 2 1/2 cups flour
- 1 teaspoon baking powder
- 1 teaspoon salt
- Extra flour
- Valentine cookie cutter
- A rolling pin with a stockinette cover
- Paper plates

### Directions

Pull up each child's sleeves and let them kneel on chairs. Tie an apron on each child, as high up as it will go to cover as much of their shirts as possible.

Measure the shortening, sugar, eggs, and vanilla into the large bowl. Let the children help with the measuring. Use an electric mixer to blend the ingredients thoroughly, or let the children mix them with a wooden spoon. Wooden spoons are nice to use because the shortening and eggs don't slide past them, and they are not noisy.

Measure the flour, baking powder, and salt. Let the children add them to the cookie mixture. After the children have mixed the dough thoroughly, cover it, and refrigerate it for an hour or longer.

A smooth plastic cloth on your kitchen table makes a good place to roll out the dough. Put a small pile of flour in front of each aproned child, and let him smooth it around on the tabletop. Give him a portion of dough.

Help the children roll their dough 1/4 inch thick. Show them how to use the cookie cutter to cut the dough. Use a wide spatula to transfer the cookies to an ungreased baking sheet.

Sprinkle them with red sugar, if desired. To make your own red sugar, put a cup of granulated sugar in a plastic bag. Add a drop or two of red food coloring, close the bag tightly, and shake hard.

Bake in a preheated oven at 400°F for 6 to 8 minutes, or until the cookies are lightly browned around the edges.

While waiting for the cookies to bake, give everyone a paper plate and a pencil. Ask each child to print his or her name on a plate so each person can have his own cookies to eat and share.

When the cookies are done, pop them onto the children's plates to cool.

## HEART-SHAPED PIZZA

Another Valentine's treat which you can serve for lunch or a snack, is a heart-shaped pizza (Fig. 2-5).

Fig. 2-5. A Heart-shaped Pizza.

## Skills to Teach

Teach children 2 years old and up:

- To sit still, listen, and follow directions
- How to grease a pan and spread dough
- How to measure, stir, and bake

Teach children 6 years old and up how to shred cheese.

## Materials List

- A large jelly roll pan
- A large bowl and a wooden spoon
- 1 cup warm water
- 1/2 cup powdered milk
- 1 package active dry yeast
- 1 tablespoon sugar
- 1 1/2 teaspoons salt
- 2 1/2 cups flour
- 1/2 pound (8 oz.) mozzarella cheese
- 1 pound ground beef
- 1 cup tomato sauce, spaghetti sauce, or pizza sauce
- 1/2 teaspoon oregano

## Directions

Show the children how to grease the jelly roll pan by spreading shortening on it with their hands. They can write letters and numbers on the greased pan with their fingers if they are not in a hurry to eat.

Help the children measure the warm water, powdered milk, yeast, sugar, and salt into the bowl. Let the children take turns stirring the mixture with the wooden spoon.

Help the children add 2 1/2 cups of flour. Let them stir it vigorously until the dough is smooth and falls away from the spoon in sheets. Add more flour until the dough loses its stickiness. Turn it onto the greased pan.

Let the dough sit for 10 minutes so it can rise slightly. Oil the children's hands and let them push and spread the dough into as large a valentine shape as possible. Pinch up the edges to hold the pizza filling.

Pour the tomato sauce on the dough. Let the children spread it to the edges of the dough with their fingers.

Crumble and fry the ground beef until it loses its redness. Drain off the fat. Spoon the meat on top of the tomato sauce. Sprinkle with oregano.

Bake in a preheated oven at 425°F for 20 minutes, or until the crust is brown, and the pizza is bubbly.

While the pizza is baking, shred the cheese. Children 6 years old and up can do the shredding, but younger children will shred their fingers along with the cheese.

After the pizza is browned, remove it from the oven and sprinkle it evenly with the cheese. Return it to the oven until the cheese melts. Heart-shaped pizza tastes good cold as well as hot.

## GIANT FAMILY VALENTINE

Hang the Giant Family Valentine with a red ribbon or yarn to surprise a special person, whether it be a teacher, a principal, or a mommy and daddy.

## Skills to Teach

Teach children 2 years old and up:

- The colors *red* and *white*
- The meaning of *large* and *small*
- Drawing and gluing skills
- How to write his or her name

Teach children 4 years old and up:

- Cutting skills
- How to create something nice for someone else

## Materials List

- White poster board. (Look in the school supplies section of your drugstore.)
- Red poster board
- Scissors
- Glue
- Water-based markers
- Red ribbon or yarn

## Directions

The children and you should decide who will

receive the Giant Valentine. Leave the white poster board flat to form the card. Cut the red poster board into a giant valentine. Use the red scraps to draw small valentines.

Children 4 years old and up can cut out these *small red* valentines and glue them into the *large white* poster board. You must do the cutting for younger children.

Let each child draw on the Giant Valentine, write messages on it, and sign his or her name.

Punch or cut a hole in each top corner. Tie on the red ribbon or yarn to hang it, or tape it to the wall or door.

---

### NOTE

Along the same line as the Giant Family Valentine is the Welcome Home Sign which can be made from any large piece of plain paper—the larger the better. Whenever a family member is away from home for a night or two, a Welcome Home Sign and maybe a cake or cupcakes can become a nice tradition. It makes that person feel very special.

In our family we make a sign when Daddy goes on business trips, when a child goes to camp or visits a relative for a week or so, or when someone returns from a hospital stay. Sometimes the children add a favorite magazine cutout to the sign, sometimes they draw pictures on it, and sometimes they write happy messages, depending on their ages. Then they tape it to the front door or to the wall just inside the door. If we bake a cake we leave it on the kitchen table and have a party when our special person comes home.

---

### VALENTINE BAG

Valentine Bags are great to use to carry the valentines the children have made for friends, to carry pastel candy hearts from the store, or to carry cookies they have baked (Fig. 2-6).

### Skills to Teach

Teach children 2 years old and up:

• The colors *red, white,* and *pink*

- The meaning of *top* and *bottom*
- Gluing skills

Teach children 4 years old and up cutting skills.

### Materials List

• White pastry bags from a supermarket bakery shop. (Brown sandwich bags will do if you can't get the white ones.)
• Red, white, and pink construction paper
• Water-based markers or crayons
• Pencils
• Scissors
• Glue

### Directions

Before beginning this craft, cut out lots of small valentine hearts from the red, white, and pink construction paper. For children 4 years old and up, trace or draw valentines on the construction paper for them to cut out.

Say to the children, "Here is a *white* bag and a pencil for each of you. Please write your name on the *bottom* of the bag so we will know it's yours." Help each child print his or her name on the bottom of the bag, using uppercase and lowercase letters.

Now tell the children, "Open your bag at the *top*. You can decorate it by gluing valentines on it and drawing on it."

### VALENTINES-AND-STRAWS JEWELRY

Valentine's Day can become even more of a celebration if the children can "dress up" with special jewelry made special for that day (Fig. 2-7).

### Skills to Teach

Teach children 2 years old and up:

• The colors *red* and *white*
• How to thread small things on a needle. (This step is very good for developing eye-hand coordination and small motor skills.)

### Materials List

• Red construction paper
• Skinny red-and-white-striped drinking straws

Fig. 2-6. A Valentine Bag.

- A large plastic needle for each child
- Red or white embroidery thread or yarn
- Scissors

### Directions

Pleat the red construction paper into folds 1/2-inch wide. Cut out many small valentines at one time.

Snip the drinking straws into 1/2-inch pieces. Hold a bunch of straws together and cut them with scissors while both hands and the straws are inside a single plastic bag to prevent the snipped pieces from flying all over the place.

*Tie* a 26-inch piece of yarn or embroidery thread onto a needle for each child. Tie a piece of snipped straw on the other end of the thread or yarn to keep the necklace pieces from falling off of it.

Tell the children to thread the *red* valentines by pushing the needle through the center of each one. Show them how to alternate the paper valentines with the *red-and-white-striped* straws until the thread is filled.

Remove the needle and tie the ends of the necklace together. Make a bracelet the same way, using a 12-inch piece of yarn.

The children can make two bracelets and hang them over their ears, for earrings!

Fig. 2-7. Valentines-and-Straws Jewelry.

## PAPER HATCHET

George Washington was born February 22, 1732, at Bridges Creek, Virginia. When he was about 6 years old he received a hatchet with which he chopped and killed one of his father's prize cherry trees. His father asked who had killed the tree, and in the story that has become legend, young George stepped forward to take his punishment. "Father," he said, "I cannot tell a lie. I chopped the cherry tree."

He did not say, "I chopped *down* the cherry tree." Actually, he chopped the bark off, and it took awhile for the tree to die. This small incident in history gives us ample excuse to lecture children on the virtues of being honest, since George Washington grew up to be our first president and the father of our country.

With a Paper Hatchet, the children can practice "chopping" without destroying anything (Fig. 2-8).

### Skills to Teach

Teach children 2 years old and up:

- The colors *yellow* and *brown*
- The meaning of *between*
- How many make *2*
- Some facts on American History
- Gluing skills
- How to write his or her name

Teach children 4 years old and up cutting skills.

### Materials List

- A popsicle stick for each hatchet
- A ballpoint pen
- Yellow construction paper
- A brown water-based marker
- Scissors
- Glue

34

Fig. 2-8. The Paper Hatchet.

### Directions

Use the pattern in Fig. 2-9 to trace two hatchet blades on yellow construction paper for each child. Cut them out for younger children, but encourage children 4 years old and up to do their own cutting.

Give each child a popsicle stick with instructions to write his or her name on it with the ballpoint pen, pressing down hard.

Tell the children to color the popsicle stick *brown* with the *brown* water-based marker. They will be able to read the name through the brown stain. Water-based markers, incidentally, are nice to use with children because the bright colors wash off hands, faces, clothes, and plastic tablecloths.

Give two hatchet blades to each child. Tell them the story of George Washington and his father's cherry tree. Then add, "To make a toy hatchet like George Washington's real one, glue the two *yellow* hatchet blades together with the popsicle stick *between* them.

Let the hatchets dry before the children practice chopping with them.

YELLOW

Fig. 2-9. The pattern to make Paper Hatchet.

Fig. 2-10. Paper Cherries.

## PAPER CHERRIES

Paper cherries can be pinned to a child's shirt or taped to a door or wall in honor of Washington's birthday (Fig. 2-10).

### Skills to Teach

Teach children 2 years old and up:

- The *circle* shape
- The letter *V*
- The colors *red* and *green*
- How many make *2* and how many make *3*

Teach children 4 years old and up cutting skills.

### Materials List

- Red and green construction paper
- A pipe cleaner for each child
- A green water-based marker
- Scissors
- Glue

### Directions

Use the pattern in Fig. 2-11 to draw two circles on red construction paper and three leaves on green

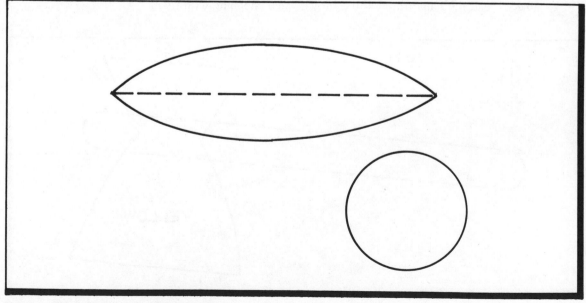

Fig. 2-11. The pattern to make Paper Cherries.

construction paper for each child. Cut them out for the younger children, but encourage those 4 years old and up to cut their own.

Give each child a pipe cleaner, two circle cherries, and three leaves. The children should color their pipe cleaners *green* with the water-based marker.

Tell the children the following: "Bend your *green* pipe cleaner in half to make the letter *V*.

"How many *red circles* do you have? Let's count them out loud." Count the red circles with the children. Then continue, "Glue one *red circle* on each end of the *green* pipe cleaner to make cherries.

"How many *green* leaves do you have? Let's count them together." Count them with the children. "Now glue the *three green* leaves to the pipe cleaner where it bends. Make the leaves stick up so they look like real ones."

## CHERRY REFRIGERATOR MAGNET

Another way to celebrate George Washington's Birthday is with Cherry Refrigerator Magnets (Fig. 2-12). The children can add them to the collection of Pom-pom Critter Magnets already on the refrigerator door.

### Skills to Teach

Teach children 2 years old and up:

- The colors *red* and *green*
- The letter *V*
- Gluing skills

Teach children 4 years old and up:

- To follow directions
- To create a useful craft in honor of Washington's birthday

Fig. 2-12. The Cherry Refrigerator Magnet and pattern.

## Materials List

Except for the glue, everything for this craft must be purchased in a craft store. Just ask for these things by name:

- Green felt
- 2 red pom-poms, size 5/8", for each child
- 2 1/4" green cloth-covered stem wire
- 1/2" wide flexible strip magnet, cut into 1" pieces
- A little glue poured into jar lids

## Directions

Use the pattern in Fig. 2-12 to trace the three-leaf shape on green felt. Cut out a shape for each child.

Give each child the leaf shape, two pom-poms, a 2 1/4-inch piece of stem wire, and a 1-inch piece of magnet.

Tell them the following: "First, bend the *green* stem wire in half so that it looks like the letter *V*.

"Next, dip each end of the wire in glue and stick it into a *red* pom-pom.

"Now glue the *green* leaf shape to the bend in the *green* wire.

"Remove the paper backing from the magnet and stick it to the back of the leaves." The magnet will stick by itself. Use the Cherry Refrigerator Magnet to hold up notes or drawings on metal appliances.

Barbara

# 3: March Crafts

The windy month of March makes us think of kites and approaching Spring. The children can make kites and fly them on the coat closet door. They can make Pinwheel Flowers before the first crocus blooms. Spring can arrive indoors even if it doesn't outdoors.

## MARCH MARCHES INTO THE HOUSE

Personally, March reminds me of mud. Maybe that's because I have four children, a cat, and a dog, and that's what they track in all month.

Fighting March mud is a constant battle. I tried putting newspapers by the front door for the children's boots, and they thought they were supposed to lay on the floor and read. The dog thought he was being paper trained again.

We lived in a house in Illinois that had red carpeting and the mud was black. Then we moved to a house in Georgia that had black carpeting; the mud there is red. March crafts keep the children indoors and out of the mud.

## CRAFT-TRAINING SKILLS TO LEARN

With this month's projects, the children again encounter plenty of colors, shapes, and cooking crafts. One craft is especially for older children—the Butterfly—and one will help younger children learn to cut with scissors—the Pot of Flowers.

Use March crafts to teach the following skills:

- Learning the names of colors
- Learning the basic geometric shapes
- How to cut, glue, color, paint, tie, and use tape
- How to print his or her name
- Learning the meaning of *on top of*
- How to use lacing cards, another good coordination exercise
- How to put things together, also called assembling skills
- How to create with dough, which is just like clay
- For older children, using a ruler to draw and measure

• Learning the meaning of *first* through *sixth*

## HANG-UP KITE

Bring Spring into the house with brightly colored Hang-Up Kites (Fig. 3-1).

### Skills to Teach

Teach children 2 years old and up:

• The colors *red, yellow, blue, pink, black,* and *green*

• The *diamond, circle,* and *triangle* shapes

• The meaning of *on top of*

• Gluing skills

Teach children 4 years old and up:

• Cutting skills

• How to tie. (Sometimes 3-year-olds can tie, too.)

• The meaning of *first* through *sixth*

### Materials List

• A large piece of paper for each kite. (Grocery bags work well, or use computer or construction paper.)

• Red, yellow, blue, pink, black, and green construction paper

• Red yarn 24″ long

• 4 pieces of ribbon or cloth for each kite, cut into strips 1 1/2″ × 6″

• Scissors

• Glue

### Directions

For each kite, open the side and bottom seams of a large paper grocery bag, if that is what you decide to use, so that it will lay flat. Using a ruler, draw a diamond shape on the bag, making each side of the diamond 12 inches long.

Cut the diamond out for younger children. Encourage children 4 years old and up to cut their own diamond.

Using the patterns in Figs. 3-2 and 3-3, trace the following on construction paper: two blue eyes, two black eyeballs, two pink cheeks, two yellow hairs, a green nose, and a red mouth. Again, cut these shapes out for younger children, but encourage older children to cut their own.

Say the following to the children, "Your kite is shaped like a *diamond*. What shape is it? A *diamond*!

*First,* glue the *blue circle* eyes on the *diamond*.

"*Second,* glue the *black circle* eyeballs *on top of* the *blue circle* eyes.

*Third,* glue the *red* mouth on your *diamond*." Help everyone glue these pieces in their proper places.

"*Fourth,* glue the *green triangle* nose on the *diamond* kite.

Fig. 3-1. The Hang-Up Kite.

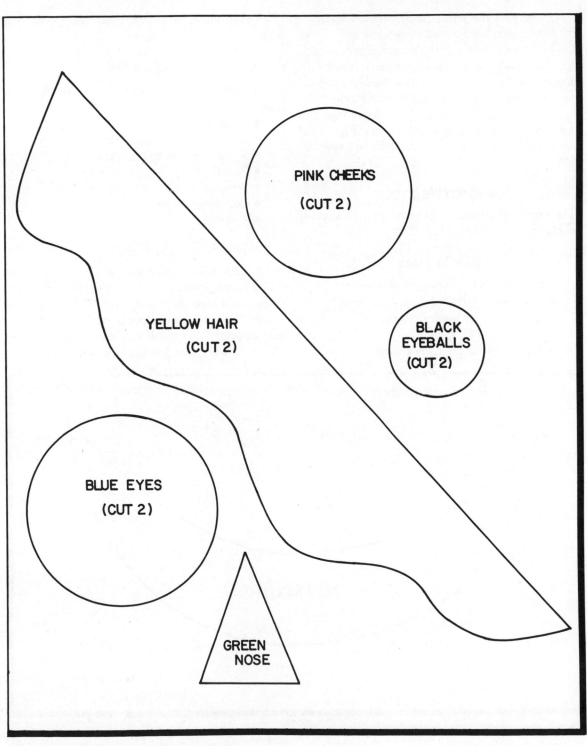

Fig. 3-2. The patterns to make the Hang-Up Kite.

*Fifth,* glue the *yellow* hair on the *diamond.*
*Sixth,* glue on the *pink circle* cheeks."

Make a small hole in the bottom corner of each kite. Each child can tie his or her piece of *red* yarn through this hole. Then he can tie the four strips of cloth at intervals along the yarn to create a kite tail.

To decorate for windy March days, tape the kite onto a door or wall at an angle as if the wind were blowing it, with the tail streaming along behind.

## PINWHEEL FLOWER

This Pinwheel Flower will also bring a burst of Spring into your home (Fig. 3-4).

### Skills to Teach

Teach children 2 years old and up:

- The colors *yellow, brown,* and *green*
- The *circle* and *square* shapes
- How to use tape
- How to write his or her name

Teach children 4 years old and up cutting skills.

### Materials List

- Yellow, brown, and green construction paper
- Crayons
- A popsicle stick for each flower
- A green water-based marker
- Pencil
- Scissors
- Cellophane tape
- A stapler

### Directions

For each flower, use the pattern in Fig. 3-5 to draw a 6-inch square on yellow construction paper. Trace the dotted lines and the five dots onto the square. Trace the flower pot onto brown construction paper and the small circle onto green paper (Fig. 3-6). Cut these parts out for children younger

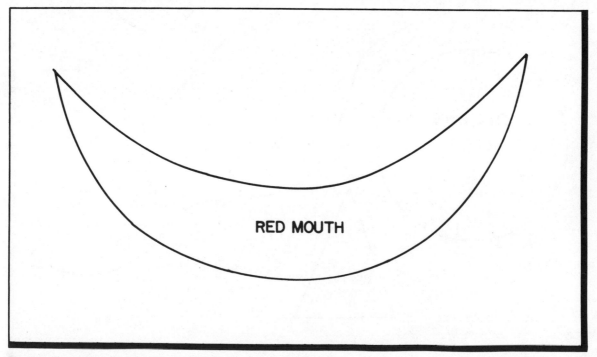

Fig. 3-3. The pattern for the kite's red mouth.

than 4 years. Encourage children 4 years old and up to cut their own.

Give each child a square, a flower pot, a circle, and a popsicle stick.

Tell them to decorate the *yellow square* on both sides with bright crayon drawings. Tell them to color the popsicle stick all over with the *green* marker.

Tell each child to print his or her name on the front of the *brown* flower pot, as neatly as possible. Make sure he holds his pencil correctly and uses uppercase, and lowercase letters. Then he can decorate his flower pot.

Cut the square on the dotted lines. Older children can cut their own. Curl the four *dotted* corners to the center of the square and staple in place, forming a pinwheel.

Next, staple the pinwheel to the end of the popsicle stick. Cut a 1/2-inch slit in the top of the flower pot.

Tell the children to insert the end of the *green* popsicle stick into the *brown* flower pot.

Give each child a piece of cellophane tape. Show the children how to tape the stick in place on the back of the pot. Add more tape if necessary.

Now they can glue the *small green circle* in the center of the Pinwheel Flower.

### BUTTERFLY

This rather complicated craft will challenge older children. When finished, they will have a beautiful butterfly that softly flaps its wings as they move the midsection up and down (Fig. 3-7).

### Skills to Teach

Teach children 4 years old and up cutting, gluing, and assembling skills.

### Materials List

• Pastel construction paper or lightweight cardboard
  • Crayons
  • Scissors

Fig. 3-4. The Pinwheel Flower.

• Glue
• Glitter

### Directions

For each butterfly trace the four pattern pieces onto construction paper or cardboard (Figs. 3-8 and 3-9). Let the children cut them out and decorate them with bright crayon drawings before putting them together.

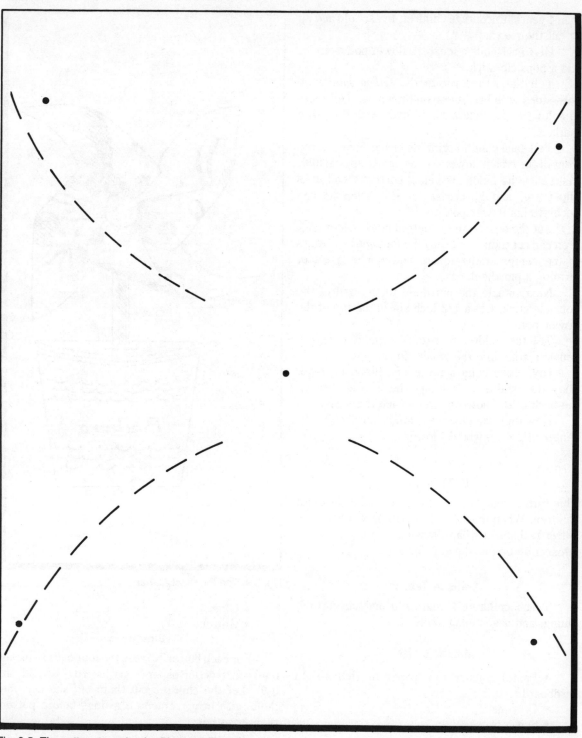

Fig. 3-5. The pattern to make the Pinwheel Flower.

The children should fasten the body to the underside of the wings by putting glue on Tabs *A* of the body (Fig. 3-9), and centering the body on the wings at Point *A* (Fig. 3-8).

Help the children fold the stick down the middle as indicated in Fig. 3-10.

Insert the body in the stick at the cut. Help the children glue Tabs *B* of the stick onto the body at Point *B*. Glue the stick shut the rest of the way down its length to make a handle.

Fig. 3-6. The pattern to make the Pinwheel Flower center and pot.

Fig. 3-7. The Butterfly.

Insert Tab *C* into Cut *C* in the midsection. Push the midsection up to the Butterfly's body as far as it will go.

The children should glue Tabs *D* of the midsection to the underside of the wings at Points *D*. Lay the Butterfly upside down to dry.

When the glue is completely dry, the children can squirt glue on the top of the wings. Hold the Butterfly over a newspaper or paper towel, and pour glitter on the glue. Shake off the excess and return it to the glitter container.

Make the Butterfly "fly" by holding the stick in one hand and gently moving the midsection up and down with the other hand. Add skinny paper antennae, or tape 1/2 of the pipe cleaner to each side of the head.

## POT OF FLOWERS

This project is designed to help younger children, as well as older children, learn to cut with scissors (Fig. 3-11).

### Skills to Teach

Teach children 2 years old and up:

- Cutting skills
- Gluing skills
- The meaning of *on top of*
- The *circle* shape
- Coloring skills

Teach children 4 years old and up cutting and assembling skills.

## Materials List

- Construction paper, different colors
- A ruler and pencil
- A stapler
- A seed catalogue or magazine with flower pictures
- Scissors
- Glue
- Tissue wrapping paper (optional)

## Directions

Tell your children to fold two sheets of construction paper in half lengthwise. Using the ruler and pencil, draw 3-inch-long lines from the folded side of the paper toward the open side. Draw ten lines at 1-inch intervals. Cut on the lines. Children 8 years old and up can use the ruler to measure and draw their own lines. Younger children cannot draw the lines, but they can cut them. Help children 2 years old and up learn to cut them with scissors.

Repeat the drawing and cutting of lines on the second sheet of folded paper. Tell the children to lay one paper *on top of* the other, with one paper raised 1 inch above the other.

Help the children hold the papers together and curl them into a *circle* with the raised paper on the inside of the *circle*. Staple the circle closed.

The children can cut and glue construction paper flowers or flowers from seed catalogues on each strip of paper that sticks up. They can use their imaginations to draw and cut out hearts, ladybugs, little pieces of crumpled tissue wrapping paper, or whatever else they want. You can also use the patterns in Fig. 3-2 to trace, cut out, and color things to glue on the pot.

The result is a very colorful and attractive Pot of Flowers that stands by itself.

## LACING CARDS

The Lacing Cards will help teach very young children shapes as well as eye-hand coordination (Fig. 3-13).

### Skills to Teach

Teach children 2 years old and up:

- The *circle, square, rectangle, triangle,* and *diamond* shapes
- Lacing skills—a very good activity to increase eye-hand coordination and small motor skills

## Materials List

- 5 or more styrofoam meat trays
- Several permanent markers in assorted colors
- A ruler
- A sharp pencil
- 5 long shoelaces

## Directions

Wash and dry the styrofoam meat trays. They can be any shape and color.

Use permanent markers to draw one large shape on each tray. You can use a cereal bowl or coffee cup to draw a circle on the first tray. Use the ruler to draw a square, rectangle, triangle, and diamond on the other four trays.

Use the sharp pencil to poke holes at 1-inch intervals in the trays to outline the shapes.

Tie a knot in the end of each shoelace. Show the children how to lace around the outside of the shape.

Teach them the names of the shapes and their colors at the same time by saying, "Here's a lacing card with a *green circle* on it. Would you like to lace it?"

When a child has finished with one card, say, "You did such a good job lacing this *green circle.* What shape did you lace? A *circle*! That's right!" No, they will not think you're crazy. Yes, they will learn their colors and shapes.

When they lose interest in a particular tray, or when it breaks, just save the shoelace and design another one.

As your children become adept at lacing, you can create more complex and challenging cards by drawing pictures of cars, houses, butterflies, or whatever. They can even design their own cards with your help.

## FLOUR-SALT DOUGH

Flour-salt dough is a lot of fun because just about

WINGS

POINT D

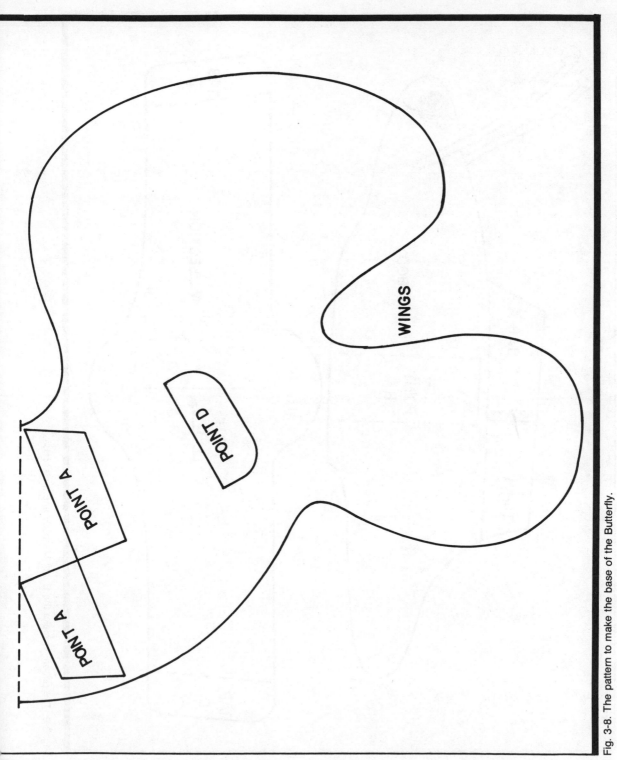

WINGS

POINT D

POINT A

POINT A

Fig. 3-8. The pattern to make the base of the Butterfly.

TAB A

BODY

POINT
B

C
U
T

TAB A

TAB
D

MIDSECTION

CUT
C

TAB
D

Fig. 3-9. The pattern to make the Butterfly's body and midsection.

| TAB C | STICK | TAB B |
| :--- | :---: | ---: |
| | | CUT |
| | ← FOLD → | |
| | | TAB B |

Fig. 3-10. The pattern for the stick to hold the Butterfly.

Fig. 3-11. The Pot of Flowers.

Fig. 3-12. The patterns for the Pot of Flowers project.

Fig. 3-13. Lacing Cards.

anything can be created from it. The children's creations become hard when they dry; so they can be kept forever. It's cheap to make; it doesn't require any special ingredients, and it cleans up easily. If anyone eats it, he or she will not make that mistake twice; so roll up their sleeves, put on painting coats, and try this project in the kitchen.

### Skills to Teach

Teach children 2 years old and up:

- How to work with dough
- How to create

### Materials List

- 4 cups flour
- 1 cup salt
- 1 1/2 cups water
- A large bowl
- A baking sheet or two
- Aluminum foil to cover the baking sheet

*The following things are optional,* depending on what the children make from the dough:

- Food colors
- Watercolors or tempera paints with brushes
- A rolling pin and cookie cutters
- Yarn for making necklaces and mobiles
- Paper clips for tree ornaments
- A garlic press or coarse sieve to make hair or fur
- Round sticks like those used in corn dogs and taffy apples to make vehicle axles

### Directions

Measure the flour, salt, and water into a large bowl. Knead by hand for a few minutes until smooth. The children will be glad to help you.

You can divide the dough into four pieces and add a few drops of red, blue, or yellow food coloring to three of them. Leave the fourth piece white. Knead in the color, then give each child a portion of dough and a small pile of flour.

The things that can be made from the dough are endless. Smaller children like to make "cookies" to feed to their stuffed animals. They make them by rolling a ball of dough and then pressing it flat on the tabletop. Bird nests with eggs are easy to make: just roll a ball of dough, make a dent in the middle to form a nest, then put several small balls in the dent to look like eggs. Roll a long coil to make a snake. They can curl a long snake around a circle of dough, building it up with more coils to make a coiled pot.

The children can use a rolling pin to roll out the dough. Then they can cut it with cookie cutters. Punch a hole in each piece before baking so the pieces can be strung with yarn to make a mobile or a necklace.

To make tree ornaments for Christmas, insert a paper clip into the top of the dough shape before it is baked. Then it can be hung after it is hard.

Older children can be quite imaginative with their creations. They can shape a Santa Claus (Fig. 3-14) and glue cotton on the finished product for a beard. To make fur from the dough, they can force it through a garlic press or a coarse sieve, lift it off with a knife, and stick it on their creation with a little water.

Making dough racing cars and trucks is a favorite with boys. First the children should shape the car or truck body and four separate wheels. Next, he should poke the wooden sticks through each wheel to make the proper hole before baking. Then he should insert the axles into the car or truck

Fig. 3-14. A Flour-Salt Dough Santa.

body. Bake the vehicle with the axles inserted in it. Keep the wheels separate during baking, laying them flat on the baking sheet. Put the wheels on the axles after they are dry. Your child will have a car or truck Fred Flintstone would envy.

To bake everything, cover the baking sheet with aluminum foil and put the dough shapes on it. Bake in a preheated oven at 225°F for many hours, depending on the thickness of the clay shape. The pieces need to dry out completely without browning. It helps to turn them over halfway through the baking. You can leave them in the oven overnight if necessary. Just remember to take them out before you use the oven to cook supper the next day.

The dried pieces can be painted with tempera or watercolors on another day. For a really fancy look, coat with clear nail polish.

---

### NOTE

The kitchen oven is used many times in this book. When several children are baking their own creations of flour-salt dough, cookies, Bake-A-Shape, or whatever, it's important to remember whose dough is whose creation. You can do this in two ways.

First, cover the baking sheet with aluminum foil. Use a black permanent marker to write the child's initials on the foil next to his or her dough.

Second, if the children are working on a project in which no foil can be used, such as most cookie recipes, use the permanent marker to write tiny initials for each child directly on the baking sheet, near the edge. Put the child's dough next to his or her initials. The writing will eventually disappear after many washings, and it will not hurt the baking sheets.

---

### TAFFY PULL

Butter everyone's hands and get ready for an old-fashioned taffy pull!

#### Skills to Teach

Teach children 2 years old and up:

- To sit still, listen, and follow directions
- How to measure
- How to write his or her name
- To count to 3

### Materials List

- 1 cup sugar
- 3 tablespoons cornstarch
- 1/8 teaspoon salt
- 1/2 cup water
- 2/3 cup honey
- A large heavy pot and a wooden spoon
- Paper plates
- Crayons
- Waxed paper

### Directions

Help the children to measure the sugar, cornstarch, and salt into the large heavy pot. As they add the 3 tablespoons of cornstarch, count to *three* with them, out loud. They can take turns mixing these ingredients until they are blended.

Help the children add the water and honey. Stir to blend.

Now take over to prevent burns. Stirring occasionally, boil the candy over high heat until it forms a hard ball when a small amount is dropped into a bowl of cold water.

Pour it onto a buttered plate. When it cools enough to be handled, give each child a glob to be pulled with his buttered hands. The children can pull it into long strings, fold it together, and pull again.

When the taffy turns white and can't be pulled any more, it is ready to eat. Give everyone a paper plate and crayons. They can decorate their plates and print their names on the front. Lay a piece of waxed paper on their decorated plates to keep their candy creations from sticking.

### ST. PATRICK'S DAY MILKSHAKE

This milkshake is simple to make. The children can put all the ingredients in a blender and turn it on and off. Just remember to put the lid on first.

#### Skills to Teach

Teach children 2 years old and up:

- How to measure and count
- How to use a blender

### Materials List

- 1 ripe banana
- 1 raw egg
- 2 cups milk
- 2 tablespoons sugar
- 1/2 teaspoon vanilla
- 3 drops green food coloring
- A blender

### Directions

Help the children measure everything into the blender container. Count the cups of milk, the tablespoons of sugar, and the drops of food coloring out loud with the children as these things are added.

Process on "high" until smooth, which should take about 30 seconds. This recipe makes about 3 cups of milkshake, but it foams a lot so it seems like more.

### CAKE MIX COOKIES

Buy the very cheapest cake mix you can find, in any flavor. Generic mixes work fine; mixes with pudding in them make delicious crisp cookies. I like to stock up on them when they are on sale.

### Skills to Teach

Teach children 2 years old and up:

- To sit still, listen, and follow directions
- How to measure, stir, and bake
- How to write his or her name

### Materials List

- 1 package cake mix
- 1/4 cup flour
- 1/4 cup water
- 1/2 cup oil
- 1 egg
- A large bowl and a wooden spoon
- Paper plates and crayons
- Waxed paper

Optional Ingredients:

- Coconut

- Raisins
- Nuts
- Chocolate chips
- Crushed peppermint sticks
- Food coloring
- Wheat germ
- Mashed banana

### Directions

Help the children measure the cake mix, flour, water, oil, and egg into the large bowl. They can take turns stirring with the wooden spoon until the dough is thoroughly blended.

Then the children can add any of the optional ingredients listed. Chocolate cake mix and nuts make a good combination, for example. For St. Patrick's Day, they can add a few drops of green food coloring and 1/4 cup coconut to a white cake mix to make green cookies.

Help the children drop the dough from a teaspoon onto an ungreased baking sheet. Place the cookies a little apart. The children can roll the dough into balls the size of a walnut, then roll each ball in granulated sugar before baking to make sugar cookies. They can roll the balls in chopped nuts, which works well with chocolate dough.

Bake in a preheated oven at 350°F for 10 minutes, or until the edges just begin to turn brown. Do not overbake.

While the cookies are baking, give each child a paper plate and crayons. Each child should decorate a "cookie plate" and write his or her name on it, using uppercase and lowercase letters. Lay waxed paper on the plates to prevent crayon from getting on hot cookies..

I don't know how many cookies this recipe makes; I've never baked a whole batch because we eat a lot of them before baking.

### NO-COOK PEANUT BUTTER BALLS

An easy treat to make, that uses no energy except the children's, is the Peanut Butter Balls.

### Skills to Teach

- To sit still, listen, and follow directions

- How to write his or her name
- How to work with dough
- How to measure, stir, and bake

## Materials List

- 1 cup peanut butter
- 1 cup light corn syrup
- 1 1/4 cups dry powdered milk
- 1 1/2 cups sifted confectioners sugar
- A large bowl and a wooden spoon
- Paper plates and pencils

## Directions

Help the children measure the peanut butter, corn syrup, dry powdered milk, and confectioners sugar into the large bowl. They can take turns stirring with the wooden spoon until everything is mixed and a stiff dough forms.

Give everyone a paper plate and a pencil. Each child should write his or her name on the bottom of the plate. Make sure they hold their pencils correctly and use uppercase and lowercase letters.

Put a portion of dough on each plate. The children can shape it into bite-sized balls by pinching off pieces and rolling them between their hands.

Smaller children who cannot make balls can make snakes. Then they can cut the snakes into segments with a table knife to make bite-sized pieces.

Leave the Peanut Butter Balls on the children's plates and refrigerate them until firm, about 1 hour.

# 4: April Crafts

April is full of rabbits in honor of Easter. Following are five bunny crafts made from paper cups, paper strips, newspapers, and pine cones, as well as a Bunny Bag in which to carry things. The children can make Easter baskets and Easter lilies, and they can use as many blown-out eggs as you want to give them.

Every year we dye tabletops, clothes, and half the kitchen towels while coloring a few dozen eggs for Easter. Then on Easter morning no one wants to eat the eggs whose whites look like a large bruise. I make these eggs into egg salad, along with the ones that someone sat on because the Easter Bunny hid them under the couch cushions.

### CRAFT-TRAINING SKILLS TO LEARN

Use April crafts to teach the following skills:

- Learning the names of colors
- Learning the names of shapes
- How to cut, glue, paint, color, and tie a bow
- Understanding the meaning of *first, second, third,* etc.
- How to draw a face
- How to print his or her name
- Counting
- How to put things together
- How to follow directions
- Learning the meaning of *upside down, fold in half, insert, overlap, top of, middle, and between*
- How to work with dough

### PLANTING SEEDS

The children can begin the Spring season by planting seeds. One of the best to plant is the marigold. It sprouts easily, grows even if overwatered, and can be transplanted to the yard or a big flower pot. It blooms all summer, and its seeds can be saved for next year.

Beans are good plants to grow, too. The children can plant the dried beans that are sold in the grocery store for cooking. Within 2 weeks they will sprout and grow leaves. Beans aren't likely to grow seed pods indoors, but the plants grow fast, they grow big, and children like them.

## Skills to Teach

Teach children 2 years old and up:

- To count to *5*
- How seeds change into plants
- That plants need water and sun to grow
- The 3 parts of a plant: the leaves, the roots, and the stem

## Materials List

- A styrofoam drinking cup for each child
- A plastic coffee can lid or shortening lid for each child
- Crayons or water-based markers
- Potting soil
- Marigold seeds or any dried beans

## Directions

Give each child a styrofoam drinking cup. They can decorate it with crayons or markers.

Poke a small hole in the bottom of the cups for drainage. Use the plastic lids as drip trays under the cups.

Fill the cups 3/4 full of potting soil. Give each child 5 seeds. Say to them, "Let's see how many seeds you have. Can you count them with me?" Count the seeds out loud with them, then ask, "How many seeds do you have? That's right. You have *five* seeds."

The children should plant the seeds in the cups, covering them lightly with 1/4 inch of soil. Help them water their seeds and place them in a sunny window. Talk with them about the fact that seeds need sun and water to grow.

Make sure that they water the seeds often enough to keep the soil moist. After about 2 weeks the seeds should have sprouted enough to show plant growth.

Pull up one of the plants when it is a few inches tall. Wash the dirt off so your children can examine the *roots*, the *stem*, and the *leaves*. Explain that the plant's *roots* drink water from the dirt. The *leaves* make food for the plant when the sun shines on them. Without water, the plant would dry up. Without sun, the plant would not be able to make food.

Each week pull up another plant until only one strong plant remains growing in each cup.

## PAPER CUP BUNNY

Any plain white paper cup will do for this craft. Generic cups make very good bunnies (Fig. 4-1).

## Skills to Teach

Teach children 2 years old and up:

- The color *pink*
- How to draw a face
- The meaning of *upside down* and *fold in half*

Teach children 4 years old and up cutting skills.

## Materials List

- A plain white paper cup for each bunny
- Permanent markers in two or three different colors
- Pink construction paper
- A white paper napkin for each bunny
- Cotton balls
- Scissors
- A small stapler (optional)

## Directions

Give each child a cup and tell them to turn the cups *upside down*. Help each child draw eyes and a mouth on his or her cup, using permanent markers. Supervise closely since these markers don't wash off.

Trace and cut out two ears from pink paper for each bunny (Fig. 4-2). Children 4 years old and up can cut their own, but you should do the cutting for a younger child. Help them glue the *pink* ears to the back of the Bunny's head, or staple them on with the small stapler.

Use a sharp pencil to make a hole in each cup where the nose should be. Make the hole small, just big enough for the tip of the child's finger.

Use a white napkin for each dress. Show your children how to *fold* the napkin *in half*. Cut three small holes on the fold (Fig. 4-2).

Your children can glue a cotton ball to the back of the napkin dress for a bunny tail.

Fig. 4-1. The Paper Cup Bunny.

To make the Paper Cup Bunny work as a puppet, a child can stick his pointer finger through the middle hole in the napkin, then poke the finger through the hole in the cup to make the Bunny's nose. He can stick his thumb through one of the remaining napkin holes, and his pinkie finger through the other hole to make paws.

Children can make "designer dresses" for

CUT   ON   FOLD

Fig. 4-2. The pattern for the Paper Cup Bunny's ears.

their puppets by decorating different napkins with water-based markers. Put newspaper under their work. They can even make a wedding veil by putting a napkin over the Bunny's ears.

### BUNNY BAG

Girls fill their bags with everything from doll clothes to secret messages. Boys usually fill their bags with little cars (Fig. 4-3).

### Skills to Teach

Teach children 2 years old and up:

- The color *yellow*
- The *rectangle* shape
- How to draw a face

- How to write his or her name

Teach children 4 years old and up:

- Cutting and gluing skills
- How to put something together (assembling skills)
- The meaning of *overlap*

### Materials List

- 2 sheets of yellow construction paper for each child
- A ruler and pencil
- Scissors
- Glue
- Transparent tape
- A paper punch

6 1/2-×-12-inch rectangle on yellow paper. See A in Fig. 4-4. Draw another rectangle 4 × 12 inches on yellow paper. (See B.) This second rectangle is the Bunny's head. To make his ears, draw a 5 1/2-inch V shape in one end of rectangle (B), as shown in Fig. 4-4. Round off the tips of the ears.

Cut these shapes out for younger children; those 4 years old and up can cut their own.

Help the children position the head (B) halfway down rectangle (A), as shown in C in Fig. 4-4, and glue in place. Next they should *overlap* and glue the edges of (A), forming a cylinder with the head *inside* it. Press the bottom of the cylinder together and tape it securely to form a bag.

The children can draw rabbit faces on the Bunny Bags, as shown in Fig. 4-3.

Use the paper punch to make two holes in the back of each bag, near the top, one on each side of the Bunny's head.

Tie a yarn handle through the holes to make a shoulder bag. A 2- or 3-year-old needs a 24-inch long handle. Bigger children need bigger handles.

Tell the children to print their names on the front of the Bunny Bag. Help them do this neatly, making sure they hold the crayon or marker correctly. They should use uppercase and lowercase letters.

The bag can be left plain, or it can be decorated with crayons, markers, or cut out flowers.

The children can glue a cotton ball on the back for a tail.

---

### NOTE

It's very important to talk to your children while they are making crafts. Follow the conversation guidewords in italics if you wish. Be very precise in describing all craft items in terms of numbers, shapes, and color.

---

Fig. 4-3. A Bunny Bag.

- Water-based markers or crayons
- Yarn 24″ long or longer
- Cotton balls

### Directions

For each bag, use a pencil and ruler and draw a

### PINE CONE FUNNY BUNNY

Many areas of the country have pine trees. If there are any near you, pick up the cones and dry them in a paper bag for a week. Then use them to make Pine Cone Funny Bunnies (Fig. 4-5).

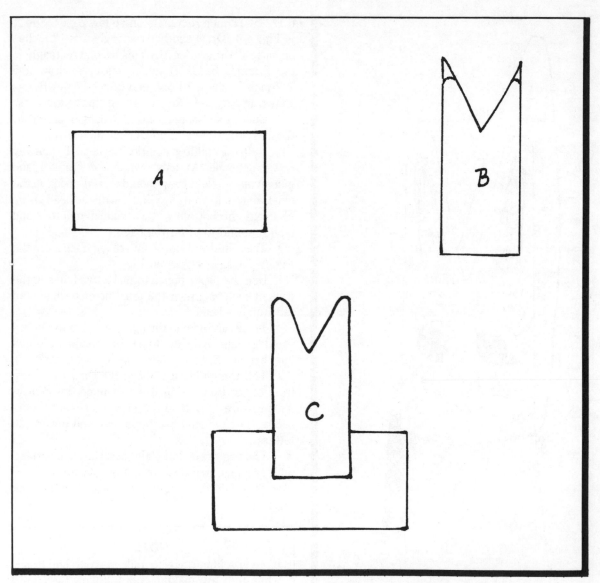

Fig. 4-4. The patterns to make a Bunny Bag.

## Skills to Teach

Teach children 2 years old and up:

- The colors *black, white,* and *pink*
- Gluing skills

Teach children 4 years old and up:

- Cutting skills
- How to put something together
- The meaning of *first* through *eighth*

## Materials List

The first six items must be purchased in a craft or fabric store.

- A 1 1/2″ white pom-pom for each child
- 3 1/2″ pink pom-pom for each child
- A 3/8″ black pom-pom for each child
- Λ 12″ pipe cleaner for each child
- Movable paste-on eyes, size 10 MM, 2 for each child

- Pink felt
- Scissors
- Glue
- Cardboard
- A pine cone, 2″ or taller for each child

### Directions

Draw the Funny Bunny feet onto cardboard. Cut it out for younger children; encourage children 4 years old and up to cut their own. Draw two paws on the pink felt for each bunny and cut them out.

Give each child a pine cone, a foot, two paws, a white pom-pom, three pink pom-poms, a black pom-pom, a pipe cleaner, and two eyes. Then tell them the following:

"*First*, put the *white* pom-pom in the middle of the pipe cleaner.

"*Second*, cross the ends of the pipe cleaner over and twist the pipe cleaner tightly around the *white* pom-pom to hold it in place.

"*Third*, bend the end of the pipe cleaner in half and twist them shut to form ears.

"*Fourth*, glue on the eyes, the *black* nose, and two *pink* pom-pom cheeks.

"*Fifth*, glue the head onto the top of the pine cone. If the pine cone is too pointed, break off the tip to make a place for gluing on the head.

"*Sixth*, glue the *pink* paws on the front of the pine cone.

"*Seventh*, glue the cardboard foot to the bottom

Fig. 4-5. The Pine Cone Funny Bunny.

of the pine cone so the Funny Bunny will stand up.

"*Eighth*, glue the last *pink* pom-pom to the back of the Pine-Cone Funny Bunny for a tail."

## PAPER STRIP BUNNY

Another bunny project the children can make for Easter is this Paper-Strip Bunny (Fig. 4-6).

### Skills to Teach

Teach children 2 years old and up:

- The colors *white* and *pink*
- The *circle* shape

- How to draw a face
- Gluing skills

Teach children 4 years old and up:

- Cutting skills
- The meaning of *overlap, insert, top of, middle,* and *between*

### Materials List

- White construction paper
- A ruler and pencil
- Scissors
- Glue

Fig. 4-6. The Paper Strip Bunny.

Fig. 4-7. Newspaper Bunnies.

- Pink and black water-based markers
- Cotton balls

### Directions

Use the pencil and ruler to measure and draw seven strips of white paper for each bunny as follows:

- 2 strips 2″×11″
- 2 strips 1 1/2″×8″
- 2 strips 1″×7″
- 1 strip 1″×11″

Cut out these strips. Encourage children 4 years old and up to cut their own.

Help each child *overlap* the edges of one of the 2-×-11-inch strips, gluing it to form a circle. Slide the second 2-×-11-inch strip through the circle, at right angles to it. Help each one *overlap* and glue the edges of this strip into a circle, also to make a circle within a circle for the Bunny's body, as shown in Fig. 4-6.

Make the head in the same way, using the two 8-inch strips. Keep the head and the body separate until the final step.

Help your children bend each 7-inch strip in half and glue the ends together to make two ears.

They should *insert* the ears into the open places on the back of a Bunny's head, glue them into place, and bend them up.

Tell them to look at the picture of the Paper Strip Bunny and draw a face with *circle* eyes, a *triangle* nose, and a smiling mouth. They can color the ears *pink* with a marker.

To make the Bunny's paws, help each child to bring both ends of the 1-×-11-inch strip to the *middle* of the strip, making a bow shape.

Help them *insert* the paws into the *top of* the body by gluing them *between* the 2-×-11-inch body strips.

Now they can glue the head onto the body, and add a cotton ball tail. Flatten the Bunny's body a little so it will stand by itself.

### NEWSPAPER BUNNIES

Decorate a string of dancing bunnies for a springtime door or window (Fig. 4-7).

### Skills to Teach

Teach children 2 years old and up:

- How to draw faces
- To count to *8*
- Coloring skills

Teach children 4 years old and up cutting skills.

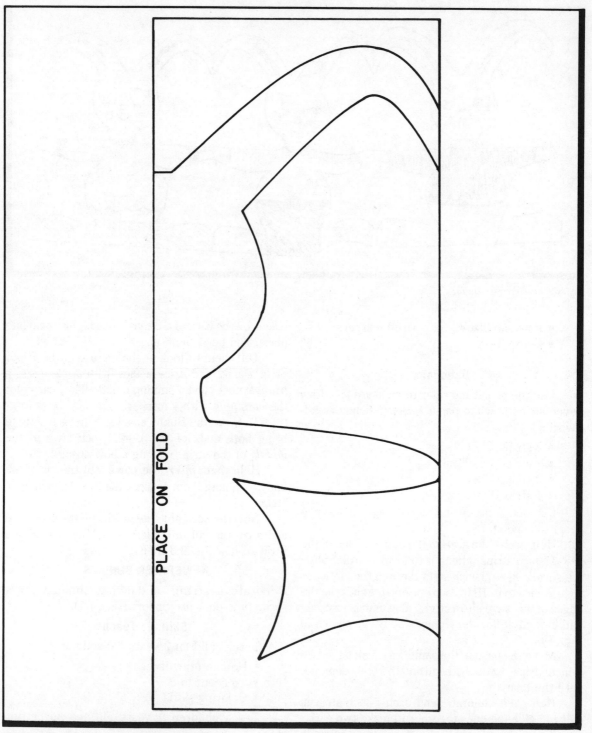

Fig. 4-8. The pattern for Newspaper Bunnies.

Fig. 4-9. Paper Easter Lilies.

## Materials List

- A large sheet of newspaper for every two bunnies
- Water-based markers and crayons
- Scissors
- Transparent tape

## Directions

Fold each sheet of newspaper into 1/4 its original size. Now fold it into 3 1/4-inch wide pleats.

For each child, trace a Bunny pattern in Fig. 4-8 on the folded paper so that the middle of the rabbit, as well as its ear, paw, and foot are laying against the folds. Do not cut these folds.

Cut out the Bunny through all layers of newspaper. Children 4-years-old and up can try cutting their own, but will need help. Unfold. You have

made eight Bunnies, enough for two children.

Say to the children, "Look how many bunnies we have! Let's count them to see how many there are." Count the Bunnies out loud with the children. Then ask, "How many bunnies are there? *Eight*! There are *eight* Newspaper Bunnies."

The children should decorate their Bunnies with crayons or markers, trying to make each one different from the next, and drawing a face on each. When they are finished, you can tape the Bunnies together into a long line before hanging them up for display.

### PAPER EASTER LILIES

These paper flowers look almost as good as real ones when they're stuck in a vase or held in the hand of the child who made them (Fig. 4-9).

### Skills

Teach children 2 years old and up:

- The colors *white, yellow,* and *green*
- The *rectangle* shape
- To count to *3*
- Some facts about nature

Teach children 4 years old and up:

- Cutting and gluing skills
- To follow directions
- The 3 parts of a flower: *petals, stamen,* and *stem*

### Materials List

- White typing paper or construction paper
- Yellow and green construction paper
- A ruler and pencil
- Scissors
- Glue

### Directions

For each child, trace a lily shape onto white paper and the stamen onto yellow paper (Fig. 4-10). Fold the yellow paper so the three stamen can be cut at the same time.

Use the ruler and pencil to draw a green rectangle 1 1/2 × 8 inches for a stem. Draw two lines 1/2 inch apart all the way down the stem. Use

—(CUT 3)

Fig. 4-10. The pattern for the Paper Easter Lilies.

them to show the children how to fold the stem into thirds to make it strong and narrow.

Cut these things out for your younger children; children 4 years old and up, can cut their own.

Tell the children the following directions:

"*First*, curl the *white* lily into a funnel shape and glue it." They will need help with this step. "The *yellow* stamen is the part of the flower that makes pollen. Bees feed pollen to their babies so the baby bees can grow. How many *yellow* stamens are you going to glue inside the lily? Let's count them and see." Count the stamens out loud together.

"*Second*, put a little bit of glue on the bottom half of the *yellow* stamens. Glue the *three yellow*

stamens to the inside of the lily so that a little bit sticks out.

"*Third*, fold the *green rectangle* along the lines that are drawn on it. This is the *stem* of the lily.

"*Fourth*, stick the pointed bottom of the lily into the end of the *green stem*. Glue the *green stem* shut all the way down."

Let the flower dry thoroughly to prevent the lily from falling out of the stem. The children can make three or four of these flowers to present to someone they love.

### EGG CARTON BASKET

Another way to prepare your children for Easter is by helping them make Egg Carton Baskets. You can make three baskets from each egg carton if you cut carefully (Fig. 4-11).

### Skills to Teach

Teach children 2 years old and up:

- Drawing skills
- The letter *U*

Teach children 4 years old and up:

- The meaning of *first* through *sixth*
- How to tie a bow

### Materials List

- Styrofoam egg cartons
- Pipe cleaners
- Narrow ribbon
- Easter grass
- Jelly beans
- Scissors
- Water-based markers and a ballpoint pen

### Directions

Cut the lids off the egg cartons. Discard them or give them to the children to use as a sandbox toy. They also make nice boats for small dollies in the bathtub.

Cut the remaining part of the cartons into three baskets of four egg cups each. Trim with scissors to make them look neat. Give each child a basket, a pipe cleaner, and a 10-inch piece of narrow ribbon.

Help the children follow these directions:

"*First*, bend the pipe cleaner so that it looks like the letter *U*.

"*Second*, push the sharp ends of the pipe cleaner through the top of the styrofoam egg basket, about 1 inch apart.

"*Third*, turn the basket over, and bend the two

Fig. 4-11. An Egg Carton Basket.

Fig. 4-12. Blown-Out Eggs.

ends of the pipe cleaner to make a tiny foot on each one.

"*Fourth*, turn the basket back over. Pull the handle up gently until the feet catch and hold.

"*Fifth*, decorate the basket." Give them water-based markers and a ballpoint pen.

"*Sixth*, tie the ribbon into a bow on the handle."

Fill the egg cups with a little bit of Easter grass and lots of jelly beans. If you snip the grass into short bits with scissors, it stays in the basket better and is easier to vacuum off the floor.

## TWELVE BLOWN-OUT EGGS

Start saving those egg shells by leaving them whole! Follow these directions to blow raw eggs into a bowl whenever you are cooking with eggs. Run water into the empty shells and let them drain. Then store them in an egg carton. If your family likes scrambled eggs or french toast, or if you do a lot of baking, it won't take long to collect several dozen empty shells (Fig. 4-12).

### Skills to Teach

Teach children 2 years old and up:

- To count to *4*
- To count to *12*
- How to draw a face
- How to paint
- Gluing skills

Teach children 4 years old and up:

- How many make a dozen
- How to cut, glue, and create

### Materials List

- Old newspapers to cover your kitchen table
- 12 large raw eggs in an egg carton for each child
- Water colors and brushes
- Cups or bowls for rinse water. (Use ones that do not tip easily.)
- 2 cardboard toilet paper rolls for each child
- Cotton balls
- Narrow tipped water-based markers
- Scissors
- Glue
- Yellow yarn
- Ballpoint pen
- White paper

### Directions

Using a corsage pin or some other sharp instrument, poke a hole in one end of a raw egg. Carefully take away bits of shell to widen the hole to about 1/8 inch.

Stick a pin or a toothpick into the opening and stir the raw egg inside the shell to break the yolk so it can be blown through the hole.

Now make a tiny hole in the other end of the egg. Put this end tightly against your mouth and blow into the egg, forcing the insides to come out. Hold the egg over a bowl to keep scrambled egg off your kitchen counter.

When the shell is empty, run a stream of water into the egg and shake it dry. Continue with all 12 eggs. Store them in an egg carton until you are ready to work with the children.

Spread newspapers on the table and put a painting coat on each child. Give each child four of the eggs.

Say to them, "Here are some eggs for you to paint. How many do you have? Let's count them." Count the eggs out loud with them. Then ask, "How many eggs do you have? *Four*! You have *four* eggs to paint."

Give them the watercolors, a brush, and a shallow cup of water. Show them how to rub the wet brush on the paint and transfer the color to the egg.

Show them how to rinse their brushes so that the colors do not mix together.

They can paint the eggs in any combination of varied hues that suits their fancy. When they are finished with each one, set it in the egg carton to dry.

Put away the paints and rinse water. Give each child four more eggs and a set of water-based markers. Again help them count the eggs out loud. Then they can color the eggs all over with the markers. Stripes, dots, swirls, and other designs are easy to add with markers since the colors don't run together. Put them in the egg carton to dry, also.

Give them the last four eggs, two toilet paper rolls, scissors, glue, yellow yarn, a ballpoint pen, and white paper. Help them count the *four* eggs out loud.

Cut the toilet paper rolls into four cylinders 1 1/2 inches high. Your children should set the eggs in these.

To make a girl, cut the yarn into 16 strands 2 1/2 inches long. The children can spread glue on the top of one egg and down the sides a bit. Then they can lay 8 pieces of yarn on each side of the doll's head, adding more glue if necessary to make it

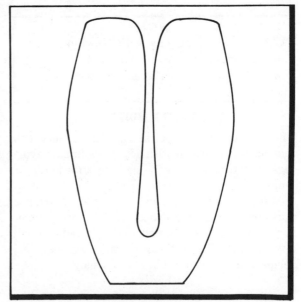

Fig. 4-13. The pattern for the ears of the Blown-Out Eggs.

stick. Help them tie this yarn hair loosely together at the bottom with more yarn to make pony tails.

They can draw a face on the egg, using narrow tipped markers. They can draw arms on the cardboard roll with the ballpoint pen, and can decorate the roll to look like a dress.

To make a rabbit, trace the ears onto white paper (Fig. 4-13). Cut them out for younger children. Encourage those 4 years old and up to cut their own.

Your children can draw a face on an egg with a narrow tipped marker. To make it look like a rabbit, they can add a triangle nose and whiskers. They should color the ears *pink*, and then glue them on the back of the rabbit's head.

They can draw paws and feet on the cardboard roll with the ballpoint pen. Then they can color the roll pink with a marker. A cotton ball can be glued on for a tail.

Repeat with the last two eggs to make another person and another rabbit, or let them make their own creations.

When all 12 eggs are decorated, admire them with your children and count them out loud together. Then ask, "How many eggs did you decorate?" *12*! You decorated a *dozen* eggs."

---

**NOTE**

Children enjoy playing with blown-out eggs, pretending they have real eggs to "cook" with. When the shells break, the pieces sweep up easily.

---

### EASTER MINTS

This is a no-cook recipe the children can mix with their hands. Flavor it with any of the liquid flavorings in the supermarket, such as strawberry or lemon.

If you want, you can instead divide it into three portions and add a few drops of food coloring to tint it yellow, red, and green. Then knead a small amount of a different flavoring into each one. This recipe makes about 1 1/2 lbs. of candy.

### Skills to Teach

Teach children 2 years old and up:

- To sit still, listen, and follow directions
- How to shape the dough
- How to print his or her name

### Materials List

- 1/3 cup soft butter
- 1/3 cup light corn syrup
- 1/2 teaspoon salt
- 1 teaspoon flavoring
- 3 1/2 cups (1 lb.) sifted confectioners sugar
- A large bowl and a wooden spoon
- Paper plates and pencils

### Directions

Help the children measure all the ingredients into the large bowl. They can take turns stirring it with the wooden spoon until it becomes too stiff. Then they can knead it with their hands. They should continue kneading until the dough is smooth.

Give each child a paper plate and a pencil. Tell them to turn their plates *over* and write their names on the *bottom* to prevent pencil lead from getting on their mints. Help them hold their pencils correctly. Make sure they use uppercase and lowercase letters.

Give each child a portion of dough on his or her plate. The children can pinch off pieces, roll them into balls, and press them *lightly* with a fork to make a fancy butter mint. Children who cannot roll the candy into balls can make snakes, cut the snakes into pieces, and press the pieces with a fork. They might eat the pieces with the fork, but that's okay too.

Leave the mints on the plates and refrigerate them for 30 minutes, until they become firm. Easter Mints taste even better the second day, if you can keep everyone from eating them all on the first day. Cover with plastic wrap and keep them in the refrigerator.

# 5:   May Crafts

Children can usually work outside during May, so painting crafts that teach color, method, and creativity are assembled in one chapter. Three puppet crafts teach everyone to follow directions while learning some very specific terms such as *above, larger, smaller,* and *first, second, third,* and so on.

### MAY CLAY PLAY

Modeling clay is like bubble gum. It's a wonderful thing for children to have, but it ruins the rug and the furniture, sticks to your shoes, and ends up stamped into the linoleum or stuck to the wallpaper.

By all means don't let this problem keep you from buying clay for your children. As with other crafts, you must first set rules and limits. Cut up an old plastic tablecloth into mats and give one to each child; discarded plastic place mats work fine, too. Seat the children at a table in the backyard. Show them how to roll, squeeze, and pinch the clay into shapes, but don't let them throw it at each other.

When they tire of the clay, save their creative pieces on a paper plate for a few days to admire them. Store the clay in a clean coffee can with a lid on it and save the mats.

### CRAFT-TRAINING SKILLS TO LEARN

Craft-training skills to practice in May repeat the same skills of past months. Children need to repeat to learn. May projects teach them the same things, but in a fresh way with each different craft.

May Craft-training skills include:

- Learning the names of colors
- Gluing, coloring, cutting, and lacing skills, which emphasize eye-hand coordination and small motor skills
- How to read and write his or her name
- Learning the basic geometric shapes
- Learning the meaning of *above, on top of, larger, smaller*
- Learning the meaning of *first* through *ninth*

### MOTHERS' DAY PLATE OF PROMISES

Ever since Anna Jarvis of West Virginia originated

Mothers' Day on May 10, 1908, we have tried to make this day special for mothers. Stores are loaded with Mothers' Day cards and presents, but nothing is quite as special as a gift made by a child who obviously adores you (Fig. 5-1).

### Skills to Teach

Teach children 2 years old and up:

- Gluing skills
- Coloring skills
- Lacing
- How to write "MOM"

Teach children 4 years old and up:

- Cutting skills
- To think of nice things to do for another person

Fig. 5-1. The Mother's Day Plate of Promises.

- Paper plates (Generic plates work very nicely)
- Water-based markers or crayons
- A hole puncher
- A colorful magazine
- Scissors
- Glue
- Narrow crimped paper ribbon
- A sheet of white paper and a pen

### Directions

Fold a paper plate in half. Cut it on the fold. Give each child 1 1/2 plates.

Turn the half plate upside down. So children can decorate them using water-based markers or crayons. Flower shapes can be cut from construction paper or from brightly colored magazine pages. They can glue these shapes on the plates and draw stems and leaves with a green marker.

Lay the half plate upside down on the whole plate, lining up the edges. Punch two holes through both plates with the hole puncher, making one hole on each side of the half plate, near the top. Tie ribbons through the two holes to anchor the half plate in position.

Now use the hole puncher to make holes 1 inch apart all the way around the plate, punching through both plates when necessary.

Starting at the top of the plate, the children can thread ribbon in and out of the holes all the way around. Tie the ribbon into a loop at the top so the plate can be hung.

Help each child think of ways in which he or she can help Mommy. Some of those ways might be: "dust the living room," "make my bed," "feed the dog," "dry the dishes," "clean my room," "sweep the porch," or anything else the child can actually do.

As the child tells you his own promises, print each one on a separate strip of paper. Let the child put his promises inside his plate. Make sure he understands that his mother can give him a strip

whenever she chooses, and he must do the task that is written on it.

Help the children write "MOM" on the front of their plates with a pen or marker. Make sure they hold the pen the right way when writing.

### CRAYON AND PAINT PICTURE

These pictures are an interesting variation to coloring with crayons. The children will be delighted at the effect (Fig. 5-2).

### Skills to Teach

Teach children 2 years old and up:

- How to use crayons
- How to use paint

Teach children 4 years old and up how to create a different effect with crayon and paint.

### Materials List

- Newspapers to cover the kitchen table
- Painting coats
- Drawing or typing paper
- Crayons
- Thinned tempera paint. (Add water to thin the paint.)
- Watercolor brushes

### Directions

Cover the kitchen table with newspapers. Pull up the children's sleeves and put a painting coat on each one.

Give them crayons and paper. They can draw, scribble, and write on the paper. Show them how to press down hard with the crayons to leave a lot of color on the paper.

When they have finished with the crayons, take them away. Give them a paint brush and the thinned tempera paint.

Children who are 4 years old and up can do this next step by themselves. Younger children will need help from you. They should paint lightly over the entire page, beginning at the top and working toward the bottom. The thinned paint will run off

Fig. 5-2. Crayon and Paint Pictures.

the wax crayon, creating an interesting effect. If the children draw with a white crayon on white paper, their design will be invisible, appearing as if by magic when they paint over it.

### POTATO PAINT PRINTS

Turn potatoes into stamps and use them to create greeting cards, party invitations, and decorated tissue wrapping paper (Fig. 5-3). They can be used to make either random patterns or pictures with a purpose.

A page full of green potato print triangles, for instance, can be turned into a forest if a brown trunk is added to each tree. A page full of red squares can be turned into a city full of houses with tiny triangle roofs.

### Skills To Teach

Teach children 2 years old and up:

• The *diamond, rectangle, square,* and *circle* shapes

• The colors *red, blue, yellow,* and *green*

• How to use a stamp

## Materials List

- Newspapers to cover the table
- Painting coats
- Raw potatoes
- A sharp knife for you to use
- A metal teaspoon for each child
- Thick tempera paint in red, blue, yellow, and green
- 4 plastic lids from cottage cheese, coffee cans, etc., for each child
- Drawing paper or typing paper

## Directions

Cover the table with newspapers. Roll up your children's sleeves and put a painting coat on them.

Cut the potatoes in half. Use the sharp knife to trim away part of the potato, making a design on the cut end. Cut a diamond on one half, a rectangle on another one, and a square on a third potato half. Leave the fourth uncut for a circle shape.

Give each child the metal teaspoon and two potato halves. They can pry out pieces of potato from the cut ends to make their own designs.

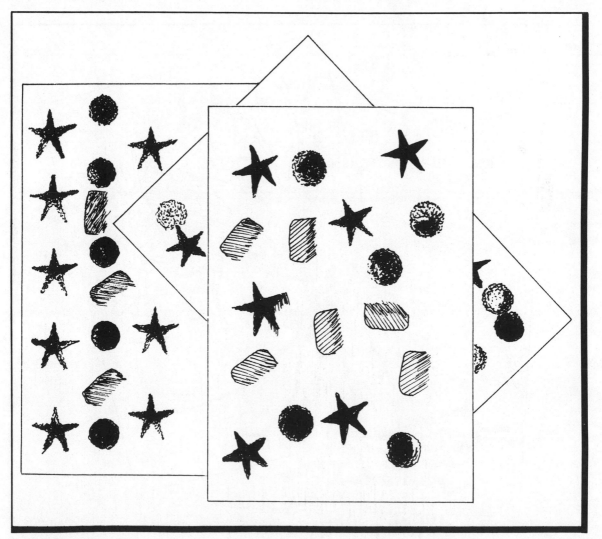

Fig. 5-3. Potato Paint Prints.

Pour a small amount of tempera paint into the plastic lids. Use a separate lid for each color.

Show the children how to dip the potato into the paint and then press it on their paper. To teach them the shapes and colors, show them how to make a *red diamond* pattern on their papers. Repeat the names of the color and shape to them as they work. For instance you can say to them, "That *red diamond* makes a pretty pattern, doesn't it?" Or, "The *diamond* stamp works well with the *red* paint." Repeat this step with the remaining shapes and colors.

## STRAW PAINTING

Children can create a unique design with just some paint, paper, and a drinking straw. They'll blow through the straw and chase the paint all over the paper to create a picture that is different each time.

### Skills To Teach

Teach children 2 years old and up:

- The names of colors
- How to write his or her name

Fig. 5-4. Straw Painting.

Teach children 4 years old and up how to create a different effect with paint.

## Materials List

- Newspapers to cover the table
- Painting coats
- Drawing or typing paper
- Pencils
- Drinking straws
- Thinned tempera paint. (Add water to thin it.)
- A teaspoon

## Directions

Cover the table with newspapers. Roll up your children's sleeves and put a painting coat on them.

Give each child paper, a pencil, and a drinking straw and ask them to write their names on the paper. Make sure they use uppercase and lowercase letters, and that they hold their pencils correctly.

Pour a small amount of thinned paint into a teaspoon. Then pour the teaspoonful on a child's paper. As you give each child the paint, tell them its color. "Barbara, this is *purple* paint. What color is it? That's right; it's *purple.*"

Tell him to aim the straw at the *purple* paint and blow hard. He can chase the little rivulets of paint all over the paper by blowing through the straw.

Next pour a different color in the teaspoon and put this on each child's paper. Tell him the color. "Now let's add *yellow.* What color is this? That's right; it's *yellow.*" He can blow the yellow paint around on the paper in the same way.

Add more colors if you wish, telling the children the name of the color each time.

## CLYDE THE CAT

Paper bags make great puppets and the children will enjoy turning them into a variety of creatures, such as Clyde the Cat (Fig. 5-5).

## Skills to Teach

Teach children 2 years old and up:

- The colors *black, white, red, green, yellow,* and *pink*
- The *circle* and *triangle* shapes
- Gluing skills
- The meaning of *on top of, above, insert, larger,* and *smaller*

Teach children 4 years old and up:

- Cutting skills
- To follow directions
- The meaning of *first* through *seventh*

## Materials List

- 2 brown paper lunch bags for each puppet
- Black, red, green, yellow, and white construction paper
- A pink marker or crayon
- A black marker or pen
- Scissors
- Glue

## Directions

For each puppet, use Fig. 5-6 to trace the following pieces on the construction paper: two white eyes, two green eyeballs, a red mouth, a black nose, and two yellow paws. Trace two ears and a tail on the second lunch bag. Cut all these pieces out for younger children. Encourage children 4 years old and up to cut their own.

Give each child a paper lunch bag and a set of Clyde the Cat pieces. Then tell them the following:

"*First,* glue the *white circle* eyes on the bottom of the closed bag.

"*Second,* glue the *green* eyeballs *on top of* the *white circles.*

"*Third,* glue the two *triangles* on Clyde's head for ears. Use the *pink* marker or crayon to color the ears *pink.*

"*Fourth, insert* the *red* mouth as far as it will go under the paper bag flap. Glue it in place.

"*Fifth,* glue the *black* nose between Clyde's eyes and 1/4 inch from the edge of the flap. With a *black* marker or pen, draw eyelashes above Clyde's eyes. Draw a straight line 1/4 inch long from the bottom of the nose to the edge of the flap. Cut a few

Fig. 5-5. Clyde the Cat and Charlie Chicken.

skinny whiskers from *black* paper and glue them on both sides of the nose." You will need to help them with the measurements.

"*Sixth,* glue the two *yellow* paws on the front of Clyde, near the bottom.

"*Seventh,* glue Clyde's tail on his back. Make it stick out by folding down a 1/4 inch flap on the end and putting glue on that only."

The children can make the puppet work by *inserting* their hand in the bag and bending their fingers so they fit into the flap. They can move their fingers up and down to make Clyde talk.

### CHARLIE CHICKEN

Another puppet the children will enjoy making is Charlie Chicken (Fig. 5-5).

### Skills to Teach

Teach children 2 years old and up:

- The colors *black, red, yellow,* and *white*
- The *triangle* and *circle* shapes
- The meaning of *on top of, above, insert, larger,* and *smaller*
- Gluing skills

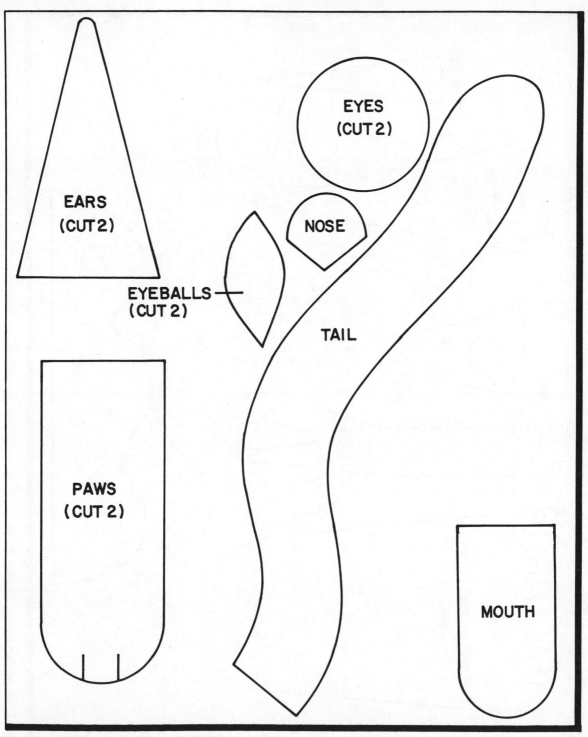

Fig. 5-6. The patterns to make Clyde the Cat.

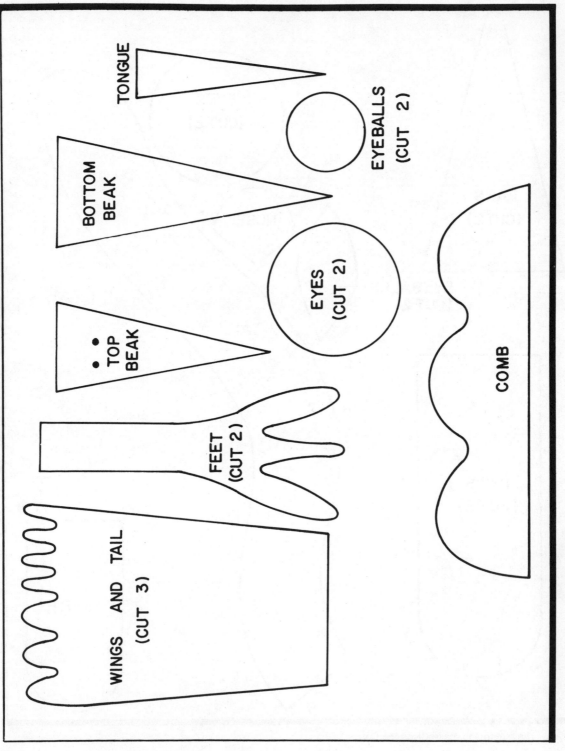

Fig. 5-7. The patterns to make Charlie Chicken.

Teach children 4 years old and up:
- Cutting skills
- To follow directions
- The meaning of *first* through *ninth*

## Materials List

- 2 brown paper lunch bags for each puppet
- Black, red, yellow, and white construction paper
- Scissors
- Glue

## Directions

For each puppet, use Fig. 5-6 to trace the following pieces on the construction paper: two black eyeballs, two white eyes, a red comb and red tongue, a yellow top beak and bottom beak, and two yellow feet. Trace the tail and two wings on the second paper bag. Cut all these pieces out for younger children. Encourage children 4 years old and up to cut their own.

Give each child a paper lunch bag and a set of Charlie Chicken pieces. Then tell them the following:

*"First,* glue the *white circle* eyes on the bottom of the closed bag.

*"Second,* glue the *black circle* eyeballs *on top of* the *white circles.*

*"Third,* glue the *red* comb *above* Charlie Chicken's eyes.

*"Fourth, insert* the *larger yellow triangle* as far as it will go under the paper bag flap. Glue it in place.

*"Fifth, insert* the *red triangle* under the flap as far as it will go. Glue it *on top of* the *yellow triangle* to make a tongue.

*"Sixth,* glue the *smaller yellow triangle on top of* the paper bag flap. Make sure it is even with the *larger yellow triangle,* forming a beak. Draw two dots for nose holes.

*"Seventh,* glue the two *yellow* feet on the front of Charlie, near the bottom.

*"Eighth,* glue two wings on the front of Charlie, *above* his feet. Let them stick out so he can fly.

*"Ninth,* glue Charlie's tail on his back. Make it

stick out by folding down a 1/4-inch flap on the end and putting glue on that only." You will need to help with the measurements.

The children can make the puppet work by *inserting* their hand in the bag and bending their fingers so they fit into the flap. They can move their fingers up and down to make Charlie talk.

## FINGER MOUSE

Another type of puppet children love is a finger puppet. Finger Mouse, shown in Fig. 5-8, will be sure to delight your children. One glove will make 5 mice.

## Skills to Teach

Teach children 2 years old and up:

- Gluing skills
- Creative play with puppets

Teach children 4 years old and up cutting skills.

## Materials List

- 2 tiny movable paste-on eyes for each puppet. (They come in packs of 32 at craft stores.)
- A ladies dress glove
- Scissors that can cut cloth
- Lightweight yarn or string
- A black permanent marker
- A pink water-base marker or crayon
- Red felt
- Glue

## Directions

Cut a 2 inch long finger off the glove as shown in Fig. 5-8, cutting a 2 1/4 inch long tail down the back of the glove.

Put a Finger Mouse on each child's finger. Help them glue on two eyes.

They can use a black permanent marker to make a nose. Help them glue on a tiny piece of red felt for a tongue.

Help the children cut the yarn into 1/2-inch pieces. They should glue two pieces on each side of the nose for whiskers.

Fig. 5-8. The Finger Mouse.

Cut two 1/2-inch rounded ears from the glove for each child. Hold them down tightly on a tabletop so the children can color one side of them with a pink marker or crayon. Help them glue them on the mouse's head just above its eyes. Press them with your finger so they stick up a little.

Slide the mouse off the children's fingers. Let them dry completely before the children play with them.

### PET PEBBLES

Children love to collect rocks and pebbles; so take them to a place where they can find a pebble to keep for a pet (Fig. 5-9). Parks and parking lots are good places to look.

### Skills to Teach

Teach children 2 years old and up:

- The meaning of *small*
- Gluing skills
- To follow directions

### Materials List

- A small, smooth pebble (about 1 1/2 inch wide) for each child
- 2 movable paste-on eyes for each child, size 3/8 inch. (Buy them in a craft store.)
- Glue
- A small box and a piece of cotton ball for each child (optional)

### Directions

Each child should select a *small* smooth rock to take home. First they must give their pet pebble a bath in the sink with soap and water. Dry it thoroughly with a paper towel or napkin.

Fig. 5-9. Pet Pebbles.

Next, they must glue two eyes on their pebble so it can see.

If they have a small box, such as the kind jewelry comes in, they can use it for their pet's bed. Glue a wisp of cotton in the bottom of the box. Lay the pet pebble on it.

## CORNFLAKE BALLS

This snack is a real treat for children. They can eat it warm or cold.

### Skills to Teach

Teach children 2 years old and up:

- To sit still, listen, and follow directions
- How to read his or her name
- How to stir and measure

### Materials List

- 1 cup peanut butter
- 1/2 cup honey
- 3 1/2 cups cornflakes
- A large bowl and a wooden spoon
- Paper plates and a marker
- Sesame seeds or wheat germ or finely ground nuts

### Directions

Help the children measure the peanut butter and honey into a small pot. Stir constantly over medium heat until blended. Remove from heat.

Microwave Directions: The children can measure the peanut butter and honey into a large microwave bowl. Microwave on high for 1 minute. Remove from oven. Let the children stir until smooth.

Help the children measure and add 3 1/2 cups cornflakes. They can take turns stirring the mixture with a spoon.

If everyone is hungry and can't wait, give them a paper plate and a spoon and let them eat while it's warm.

To shape into balls, chill the dough for 30 minutes in the refrigerator. While the dough is chilling, play the Read-Your-Name Game (See Chapter 11).

After the dough is stiff, put a portion on each child's plate. They can pinch off small pieces, roll them into balls, and then roll the balls in sesame seeds, wheat germ, or finely ground nuts.

Store these snacks in the refrigerator on the children's plates.

# 6: June Crafts

This chapter begins with a terrific Father's Day craft, which is very hard to find in other craft books. It takes a week to complete, but fathers are worth it, so start early. Several old-fashioned crafts that children have learned from and enjoyed for generations are also among this month's crafts. Clothespin Dolls, Making Paste for Cut-and-Paste Pages, and Stocking Kitty have been around since grandmother's day, at least, and Making Butter has been around since cows were discovered.

## PASTE IS A STICKY WORD

While teaching first grade, I met a young lady named Glenda who had a passion for paste—she like to eat it. We used school-issue paste that was thick, slimy, white, and had a minty smell. Glenda liked to take giant fistfuls and hide it in her desk to nibble when I wasn't looking. At least homemade paste will not be harmful to anyone's health if you happen to have a paste-nibbler in your family.

Learning to paste isn't easy for very young children since they must spread the paste on the back of the picture. They often begin by spreading paste on the front of the picture, turning the picture over to stick it to their paper, and then wondering where their picture went.

## CRAFT-TRAINING SKILLS TO LEARN

For the first time, the children are asked to print their last name as well as their first. They are introduced to *reading* the names of the five shapes, and to reading and spelling an important word to them: DAD. Many of the crafts stress the importance of cooperating and taking turns, which they must do in school later.

Craft-training skills to practice in June include:

• How to paste
• Cutting, drawing, and lacing skills
• How to spread with a knife, another eye-hand coordination skill
• Learning the names of colors
• Learning the meaning of *divide, in half, larger* and *largest,* and *smaller* and *smallest*

- Counting
- Following directions
- Shaping dough
- Measuring
- How butter and peanut butter are made
- Creative play with clothespin dolls and egg carton caterpillars
  - How to tie and braid (older children)

### DAD SIGN FOR FATHER'S DAY

Start this craft about a week before Father's Day so that everything has time to dry. Sawdust makes a big mess in the kitchen, so plan on working in the garage or outside.

### Skills to Teach

Teach children 2 years old and up:

- The colors *brown* and *blue*
- How many make *3*
- How to shape dough to form letters
- The letters *A* and *D*

Teach children 4 years old and up:

- The meaning of *divide*
- How to spell *DAD*

### Materials List

Buy the first 5 items in a hardware store.

- A piece of wood 1″ × 4″ × 6″ for each child
- Fine-grained sandpaper
- Wood stain, any color
- Clear shellac
- A 2″-wide paint brush for each child
- An old piece of cloth for each child
- Flour-Salt Dough. (See Chapter 3.)
- Blue food coloring
- Contact cement (glue)

### Directions

Give your children the wood and a piece of sandpaper. Show them how to rub the wood until it's smooth.

Spread newspapers on the work area. Put a painting coat on your children. Pour about a tablespoon of wood stain on an old piece of cloth. Give one to each child and let them rub the wood until it is colored *brown* all over.

Fig. 6-1. The DAD Sign for Father's Day.

Fig. 6-2. The Egg Carton Caterpillar.

Make Flour-Salt Dough and add a few drops of blue food coloring. Let the children knead the color into the dough. To teach the name of the color, ask them. "What color is the dough?" If they do not know, tell them. "It's *blue*." Then ask again, "What color is it? That's right. It's *blue*."

Give each child 1 1/2 cups of blue dough. Tell them to *divide* it into three equal pieces. Ask your younger child how many pieces he has. If he does not know, count the pieces out loud with him. Then ask again, "How many pieces of dough do you have? Yes, you have *three* pieces."

This step can be done at the kitchen table. Give each child a little flour to spread on the table in front of them. Help them roll the dough into three snakes, then curl and bend the snakes to form the letters DAD. Talk about the names of the letters and what they spell.

Arrange the letters on a cookie sheet covered with aluminum foil. Bake at 225°F until they are hard and dry, but not browned. You may want to leave them in a turned-off oven overnight to help them dry.

Help your children glue the baked letters onto the piece of wood, spelling DAD.

Go to the garage once more with old newspapers and painting coats. Give them a 2-inch brush and let them shellac the entire DAD Sign. Let them dry before giving them to Dad.

### EGG CARTON CATERPILLAR

A fun craft to make is this Egg Carton Caterpillar (Fig. 6-2). It teaches a variety of skills, and the children will really enjoy making it and playing with it.

### Skills to Teach

Teach children 2 years old and up:

- To follow directions
- Eye-hand coordination
- How to draw a face
- The meaning of *in half*
- The letter *V*
- To count to *7*
- To count to *6*

Teach children 5 years old and up:

- Cutting skills
- How to create a puppet

## Materials List

- A styrofoam egg carton, one for every 2 caterpillars
- Scissors
- Pipe cleaners
- Permanent markers in several different colors

## Directions

Cut the lid from the egg carton with the scissors, then discard the lid. Cut the egg cups into two strips of six cups each. Children 5 years old and up can do this cutting themselves.

Give the children an egg carton strip and 7 pipe cleaners. Say to the younger children, "Here are some pipe cleaners. Count them and see how many you have." Count out loud with them: "One . . . two . . . three . . . four . . . five . . . six . . . seven." Then ask, "How many pipe cleaners do you have? That's right! *Seven!*"

Help them push the end of a pipe cleaner through one side of an egg cup, across it, and then through the other side. They can bend down both ends of the pipe cleaner to make 2 legs. Repeat with each egg cup until the caterpillar has 12 legs.

Children 4 years old and younger may have trouble pushing the pipe cleaner through the styrofoam. To make it easier, poke two small holes on each side of the egg cut with a sharp object, such as a pencil. Then the child can thread the pipe cleaners through the holes; it's very good practice in eye-hand coordination.

There is one pipe cleaner left. Tell them to bend it *in half* so that it looks like the letter *V*. This pipe cleaner is the antennae.

Turn the caterpillar upside down. Help them push the two ends of the pipe cleaner through the top of the caterpillar's head. Turn the caterpillar back over and pull the pipe cleaners up gently as far as they will go. Fold the ends down about 1/8 inch to make them a little thicker.

Give the children permanent markers to draw big round eyes and a mouth on their creatures. Caterpillars do not have noses, but most children insist on giving them one anyway.

The markers can be used to make stripes and dots on the caterpillar's body. Ask your children how many humps their caterpillars have, including its head. Count the humps together out loud. Then ask, "How many humps does it have? That's right. *Six* humps!"

## CLOTHESPIN DOLL

This wonderful old-fashioned doll leaves lots of room for a child to pretend and create. Children who are too young to cut cloth and tie yarn won't be able to make this doll, but they do like to play with it if someone makes it for them (Fig. 6-3).

### Skills to Teach

Teach children 5 years old and up:

- Cutting skills
- Gluing skills
- How to tie yarn
- Creativity and imagination

Fig. 6-3. The Clothespin Doll.

## Materials List

- A wooden clothespin
- Narrow-tipped markers
- Yarn
- Glue
- Cloth scraps
- Sharp scissors

## Directions

Tell your children to draw a face and shoes on the clothespin, using the narrow-tipped markers.

Help them cut eight 3-inch pieces of yarn and glue them onto the doll's head for hair. They can draw hair with a marker to make a boy doll.

Tie the yarn together at the end with another piece of yarn to make two ponytails. Trim the ends and press the hair close to the head.

Help your children cut a 3-inch circle of cloth. They can measure it with a ruler or they can draw a circle, using a coffee cup as a pattern. Cut a 1/2-inch slit in the center of the circle. Slip it over the doll's feet and adjust it around the neck to make a shirt.

Cut three pieces of yarn 5 inches long. Tie them around the neck, under the shirt. Tie the yarn together at the ends with another piece of yarn. Trim to make wrists and hands.

Help your children cut a 4-inch circle of cloth. They can cut a 1/2-inch slit in the center of it and slip it over the doll's feet for a skirt.

They can make the clothes form-fitting around the waist by wrapping yarn three times around like a belt, then tieing.

Make a hat by cutting a 1 1/2-inch circle of cloth. Cut a 1/2-inch slit in it. Slip it onto the head and adjust the brim up or down.

Your children can make a large wardrobe for their dolls by using cloth scraps. They can add to their clothespin family as long as they want, and can even make them a shoe-box house.

## STOCKING KITTY

A good way to use a sock that has lost a mate is by making a Stocking Kitty. Big socks make big kitties; little socks make little kitties (Fig. 6-4).

## Skills to Teach

Teach children 2 years old and up:

- How to stuff and tie
- How to draw a face

Teach children 5 years old and up:

- How to tie a bow
- How to braid

## Materials List

- Light-colored socks
- Red and black permanent markers
- Old nylons cut into strips for stuffing
- Yarn
- Sharp scissors
- Ribbon (optional)

## Directions

Help each child stuff the entire foot of a sock with old nylons cut into strips.

Tie yarn 1/4 of the way down the stuffed section pulling the yarn tightly to form a head. Children 5 years old and up can do this step with very little help. Younger children will need you to do it for them.

The child should pull up two corners, one on each side of the head. They should tie these corners tightly with yarn to form ears.

Next they should tie yarn tightly at the bottom of the stuffing to form the body and keep the stuffing in place.

Help each child cut the sock top into three equal sections. These sections must be braided to form a tail. Tie the end of the braid with more yarn. Children as young as 5 years old can be taught to braid.

Now each child should draw a face on the Stocking Kitty with the black and red permanent markers. He can draw large front legs on the body as shown in Fig. 6-4. Color the fronts of the ears red.

If you wish, tie a ribbon around the Stocking Kitty's neck. Children 5 years old and up should be able to tie the bow themselves. If they can't, this is a good time to learn.

Fig. 6-4. The Stocking Kitty.

### MAKING PASTE FOR CUT-AND-PASTE PAGES

White glue works so well that people don't bother anymore with homemade paste, but it's nice for the children to see that everything doesn't need to be bought in a store. Flour-water paste has been around for ages, and best of all, it's cheap.

This paste is best when made up fresh. It will keep for three days before spoiling, however.

### Skills to Teach

Teach children 2 years old and up:
- Cutting skills
- Gluing skills
- How to write his or her first and last name

94

## Materials List

- 1 cup cold water
- 2 tablespoons flour
- A jar with a tight fitting lid
- A cooking pot and a wooden spoon
- A sheet of plain paper
- Old magazines with lots of pictures
- Scissors

### Directions

Measure the water and flour into the jar, closing the lid tightly. Shake it vigorously until it is smooth and no lumps remain. Pour it into the cooking pot.

Cook on high heat, stirring constantly with the wooden spoon, until the mixture comes to a boil. Reduce heat and boil 1 minute. Remove the paste from the heat and pour it onto a large flat plate to let it cool quickly. Children can use popsicle sticks to spread the paste, or they can use their fingers.

Give each child a sheet of plain paper, old magazines to cut up, and a pair of scissors. Let them cut out any pictures or scraps they like and paste them on the paper. When they tire of this activity, help each child write his or her first and last names on the front of the paper. Make sure they hold their pencils correctly and use uppercase and lowercase letters.

### STUFFED FISH MOBILE

This fish mobile could be used to decorate a bedroom, classroom, or meeting room. It can be a group project with everyone making a fish to contribute, or each person could make his own fish to hang up separately (Fig. 6-5).

### Skills to Teach

Teach children 2 years old and up:

- How to work cooperatively
- Coloring skills

Teach children 4 years old and up:

- Cutting skills
- To follow directions

## Materials List

- Newspapers
- White tissue wrapping paper
- Crayons
- Scissors
- A stapler and lots of staples
- String or yarn
- A coat hanger

### Directions

Help the children tear the newspaper into pieces about 3 inches square. They should crumple each piece to use as stuffing.

Cut a piece of tissue wrapping paper in half. Put 1/2 on top of the other, forming two layers. Draw a large fish shape on the paper. Children 6 years old and up can draw their own fish.

The children can use crayons to draw eyes, gills, fins, scales, stripes, or whatever on *both* pieces of paper so that when the fish is completed it will be decorated on both sides. Cut out the fish shape through both layers of paper at the same time. Children 4 years old and up can try cutting their own.

Starting at the head, staple around the edges of the fish. Leave the entire back half of the fish open to make stuffing easier. The children can use the crumpled newspaper to stuff the fish. Then staple the fish closed the rest of the way around.

Tie a knot in one end of a 14-inch piece of yarn to keep it from pulling through, and staple it to the middle of the fish's back.

To turn the Stuffed Fish into a mobile, tie five fish onto a coat hanger as shown in Fig. 6-5.

### LACE-A-SHAPE

The more a child actually touches and works with the five basic shapes, the more familiar he will become with them. Lace-A-Shape offers a chance to explore the shapes in a physical way, that is, by lacing around them. It encourages children to read the name of the shape and to practice eye-hand coordination (Fig. 6-6)

Fig. 6-5. The Stuffed Fish Mobile.

### Skills to Teach

Teach children 2 years old and up:

- Lacing skills
- Eye-hand coordination
- The 5 basic shapes: *circle, square, triangle, rectangle,* and *diamond*
- How to read the names of the shapes

### Materials List

- 5 styrofoam meat trays
- Permanent markers in several colors and a ruler
- 5 shoelaces
- A sharp pen or pencil

### Directions

Wash and dry the meat trays.

Use a ruler and something round, such as a drinking glass or coffee cup, to draw one basic shape on each tray with the permanent markers.

Print the name of the shape under it, using lower-case letters.

Punch holes with a sharp pen or pencil at 1-inch intervals to outline the shapes. Tie a knot in one end of the shoelaces and string a lace through each tray.

Put the finished trays in a place where the

---

### NOTE

The circle shape is easy for children to learn. Play this game along with the Napkin Game at lunchtime. Hold up an empty lunch plate and say, "This is a circle. Liz, what shape is it?"

Liz answers, "A circle."

"That's right. You get a circle plate." Hand Liz her plate and repeat with the next child. The Napkin Game can be found in Chapter 8.

---

children can work on them easily. A soft throw rug makes a nice work area. As they pick one up, teach the names of the shapes by commenting, "I see that you're lacing a round *circle*. What shape is that? Yes, a *circle*." You could also say, "You're doing a good job lacing the *diamond* shape. Can you read me the word on the card? That's right; it says, '*diamond*.'"

## HARDTACK COOKIES

This project is not only delicious, but is useful in teaching children how to measure, as well.

### Skills to Teach

Teach children 2 years old and up:

- To count to 4
- How to measure and stir

Fig. 6-6. Lace-A-Shape Trays.

- The meaning of *largest, smallest, larger,* and *smaller*

Teach children 4 years old and up the differences among 1 cup, 1/2 cup, 1/3 cup, and 1/4 cup.

### Materials List

- A large bowl
- A wooden spoon
- A rubber spatula
- Vegetable cooking spray
- 12″ × 15″ jelly roll pan
- 2 cups quick-cooking oatmeal
- 1/2 cup cornmeal
- 1/2 cup oil
- 1/2 cup honey
- 1 1/3 cups flour
- 1/4 cup brown sugar
- 1/4 cup water
- 1 teaspoon salt

### Directions

Line up four measuring cups where the children can see them: 1 cup, 1/2 cup, 1/3 cup, and 1/4 cup. Help them count the cups out loud. Tell them that they will be using all four of the cups to make the Hardtack Cookies. Encourage them to pick up and examine the four cups. Ask them which cup is the *largest* and holds the most. (1 cup) Which cup is the *smallest* and holds the least? (1/4 cup) Which cup is *larger*, 1/2 cup or 1/3 cup? (1/2 cup) Which of these cups is smaller? (1/3)

Help the children measure the oatmeal, cornmeal, oil, honey, flour, brown sugar, water, and salt into the large bowl. Let them take turns stirring the dough until it is well mixed.

Spray the jelly roll pan with vegetable cooking spray. The children can use the rubber spatula to spread and press the dough evenly until it covers the bottom of the pan.

Bake at 325°F for 30 minutes. Cut into 2-inch squares with a knife while hot and let the Hardtack Cookies cool in the pan.

This recipe makes 40 cookies. They can be frozen, or you can store them in an airtight container.

## MAKING BUTTER

The old-fashioned art of making butter is easily accomplished, and the result is delicious.

### Skills to Teach

Teach children 2 years old and up:

- Where butter comes from and how it is made
- How to work together and take turns
- How to spread with a knife

### Materials List

- 1/2 pint pure whipping cream (nothing added to it)
- A jar with a tight-fitting lid
- Table knives
- Crackers

### Directions

Cold whipping cream will not turn into butter;

Fig. 6-7. Making Butter.

so let it sit out at room temperature for about an hour. Then pour it into a jar and close the lid tightly.

The children can take turns shaking the jar as hard as they can. After a few minutes the cream will become grainy looking as the butterfat starts clumping together.

As the children continue to shake it, the butter will suddenly form as a lump, leaving the watery "buttermilk" behind.

Put the entire jar into the refrigerator until the butter becomes firm. Drain off the buttermilk, and see if anyone is brave enough to taste it. If you wish, you can instead carefully drain the buttermilk from the soft butter, putting the butter in a shallow bowl.

Give each child a table knife and a few crackers. They can spread the butter for a tasty snack.

## MAKING PEANUT BUTTER

It takes a while to shell all those peanuts. In the meantime the children learn a valuable lesson in cooperation. It would take much longer if one person had to shell the peanuts alone! It also teaches them why Mother does not make homemade peanut butter all the time; it's so much faster to buy it at the store.

### Skills to Teach

Teach children 2 years old and up:

- How peanut butter is made
- How to measure ingredients
- How to spread with a knife

### Materials List

- A 12-ounce bag of roasted peanuts in the shell (1 3/4 cups shelled peanuts)
- 1 teaspoon sugar
- 1/4 teaspoon salt
- 3 tablespoons vegetable oil
- A blender
- Rubber spatula
- A table knife for each child
- Crackers

### Directions

Help the children shell the peanuts and remove the brown, paper-thin membrane. Even 2-year-olds can help if you crack the shell for them.

Pour all the peanuts in a blender container. Run the blender on "high" until the peanuts are ground into tiny bits. Stir with a rubber spatula if necessary.

Help the children measure and add 1 teaspoon sugar, 1/4 teaspoon salt, and 3 tablespoons vegetable oil to the ground peanuts.

Run the blender on "high" again, stirring when necessary, until the peanut butter is thick and smooth. Scrape it into a bowl.

Put the bowl on the table where everyone can reach it. Give each child a table knife and crackers and let them spread their own homemade peanut butter.

Store the rest in a covered container in the refrigerator. This recipe yields 1 cup.

# 7: July Crafts

July takes the children out-of-doors to collect things of Nature for Masking Tape Nature Walk and Crayon Leaf Prints. They bring them home to make works of art and to increase their language skills at the same time.

## TEACH WHEN YOU TRAVEL

When traveling with young children, point out words to read. STOP signs are excellent to start with. Then begin reading other words along the road.

Sing nursery rhymes and the alphabet song out loud as you drive. If no one wants to chime in, pretend you enjoy singing them to yourself. You will look like you are having so much fun that soon the children will join you. If you don't know the tune, make one up. They will never know the difference. Caution: do not sing finger game songs while driving. "One Little, Two Little, Three Little Indians" can be hazardous by the time you get to "Ten Little Indian Boys."

## CRAFT-TRAINING SKILLS TO LEARN

Children should be able to follow a teacher's directions when they enter school. July crafts teach the children what the teacher means by the words *large, small, longest, shortest, in between, in the middle, pleat, fringe,* and *assemble.* They learn that if they follow directions and do steps 1, 2, and 3 as they are told, the end result will be a nice project that they can keep or eat, whichever is appropriate.

Craft-training skills to practice in July include:

- How to use descriptive words
- The shapes and how to read their names
- Learning the names of colors
- Counting
- Learning how many make a dozen
- Drawing, cutting, gluing, coloring, and writing skills.

## MASKING TAPE NATURE WALK

The Masking Tape Nature Walk is a good way to

start teaching your children about the world of nature. They will also have a memento of this time you shared.

### Skills to Teach

Teach children 2 years old and up:

- An awareness of the small things around them
- The beauty of Nature
- How to describe things
- Counting skills
- Gluing skills
- How to write numbers
- How to write his or her own name

### Materials List

- A roll of masking tape—the wider, the better
- A sheet of construction paper for each child
- Glue
- Crayons or a pencil

### Directions

Use the masking tape to make a loose bracelet around each child's wrist. Make sure the sticky part of the tape is facing *outward,* not against the skin.

Go for a walk in a park, field, or forest preserve—wherever there are trees, grass, and rocks.

Encourage your children to look for small things that can be stuck to the masking tape bracelet. They might include a pretty pebble, a feather, a tiny pine cone, an acorn, a fuzzy grass, a wild flower, and a small leaf.

As you walk along and they select their treasures, comment on each one by naming and describing it. You might say, "What a lovely pebble. It's so smooth and brown." Or, "Did you find a white feather? It wills stick to your bracelet, I bet." Or, "That's such a tiny brown pine cone! I wonder which tree it fell from." In this way you will be teaching them how to describe things in terms of color, size, texture, and place of origin.

Encourage them to take only one of each thing they find, or they may cover their bracelet with leaves and be finished very quickly. That's not the idea of the Nature Walk.

When the bracelet is full, carefully remove it from their wrists until you return home.

Once home they can make a collage from their collections by gluing them onto the sheet of construction paper.

Ask them to count the number of items they have collected. Count them out loud with each child. Then ask, "How many things did you collect?" He should tell you the number. Help him write this number on the front of his collage.

Now they should print their name on the collage, using uppercase and lowercase letters. Make sure they hold their pencil or crayon correctly for writing.

If they are interested, they can print the name of each object next to it, with your help.

### CANARY MOBILE

The children can "fly" a canary when they finish this project (Fig. 7-1).

### Skills to Teach

- The colors *yellow, orange,* and *black*
- The *circle, diamond,* and *rectangle* shapes
- Gluing skills
- The meaning of *both, large, small, longest, shortest,* and *in between*

Teach children 4 years old and up:

- Cutting skills
- The meaning of *fringe* and *assemble*

### Materials List

- Yellow, orange, and black construction paper
- A pencil and ruler
- A paper punch
- Yarn
- Scissors
- Glue

### Directions

For each mobile, use the pencil and ruler to

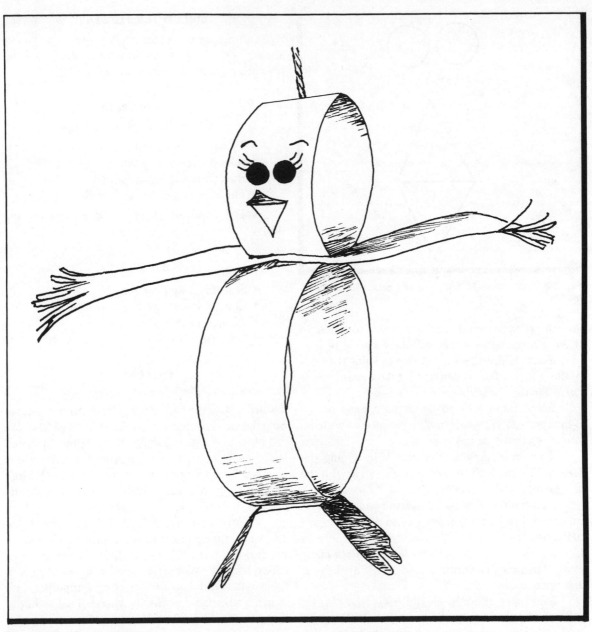

Fig. 7-1. The Canary Mobile.

measure and draw four rectangles on yellow construction paper to make the body, head, wings, and tail. Make the body rectangle 1 1/2 × 12 inches. Draw the head rectangle 1 1/2 × 9 inches. Draw the wings 1 1/2 × 8 inches. Draw the tail 1 1/2 × 3 inches.

Use the pattern in Fig. 7-2 to trace the beak and feet onto orange paper. Trace two circle eyes onto black paper. Cut out all these pieces for the younger child. Encourage children 4 years old and up to cut their own.

Tell the children to overlap the ends of the

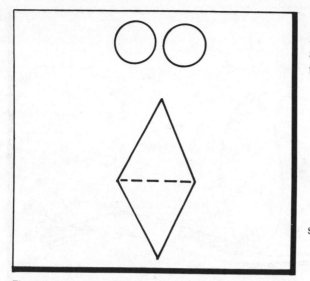

Fig. 7-2. The pattern for the eyes and beak of the Canary Mobile.

*longest yellow rectangle* and glue them together to make a *large yellow circle,* for the canary's body.

Your children should overlap and glue the ends of the 9-inch *yellow rectangle* to make a *small yellow circle* for the canary's head.

Show them how to *fringe* both ends of the 8-inch *yellow rectangle* by making small cuts with the scissors for the canary's wings.

They can *assemble* the canary by gluing the *large yellow circle* to the *small yellow circle* with the wings centered *in between* them.

Tell them to fold the *orange diamond* in half to make the beak. They can put glue on the bottom half of the beak and glue it on the canary's head where its face should be. They can glue on two *black circle* eyes. Then they can draw on eyelashes, eyebrows, and nose holes.

Now your children should *fringe* the *shortest yellow rectangle* to make the canary's tail. Glue it on the back of the canary's body, letting the fringe stick out like feathers.

To hang the canary, use the paper punch to make a hole in the top of the head. Tie a small scrap of paper to one end of a 12-inch piece of yarn. Thread the other end of the yarn through the hole. Hang the canaries in an open window to watch them fly.

## EGG CARTON FLOWERS

Egg cartons are useful for many projects, as you've already seen. Egg carton flowers are delightful as a teaching tool and a decoration (Fig. 7-3).

### Skills to Teach

Teach children 2 years old and up:

- To count to *12*
- How many make a *dozen*
- How to put things together
- The meaning of *in the middle*

Teach children 4 years old and up cutting skills.

### Materials List

- Styrofoam egg cartons
- Construction paper, any colors
- 12 pipe cleaners
- Scissors

### Directions

For each child, cut the lid off the egg carton and discard it. Cut the carton into 12 separate egg cups. Snip the sides of each cup so that it has 4 petals. You can make the petals pointed by snipping out small triangles from each cup, or you can make them rounded by cutting more carefully. Older children with pretty good cutting skills (ages 8 years old and up) can make these cups themselves.

Use the patterns in Figs. 7-4 and 7-5 to trace 12 construction paper flowers. A faster way to make the flowers is to draw four circles on a sheet of paper, using a small cereal bowl or a large cup. Cut them out. Fold two of the circles together into fourths, then cut a ruffled or rounded shape out of this quarter. Unfold, and you will have two paper flowers.

Tell the children that there are enough egg cups to make a *dozen* flowers. Ask, "How many make a *dozen*? Let's count the egg cups and find out." Count the egg cups out loud, together with the children. "One, two, three," and so on to 12. Then ask again, "How many make a dozen? Twelve! There are 12 egg cups in a dozen."

Fig. 7-3. Egg Carton Flowers.

Show the children how to use the sharp pipe cleaner to poke a hole *in the middle* of a paper flower, then *in the middle* of an egg cup.

Bend the very tip of the pipe cleaner over on the inside of the cup, to hold it in place. Make a second little bend under the paper flower to keep it from sliding down the pipe cleaner.

A 2-year-old can assemble his or her own flowers if you poke a tiny hole in the middle of the egg cups and in the paper flowers first. He will still get lots of practice in eye-hand coordination and as-sembly skills by putting the flowers together him-self.

## TISSUE PAPER FLOWERS

These flowers can be put on packages, or used as a decoration for a table or pillow. They make nice gifts for a teacher, a leader, or for someone who is sick.

### Skills to Teach

Teach children 2 years old and up:

Fig. 7-4. The patterns for Egg Carton Flowers.

Fig. 7-5. Another pattern for Egg Carton Flowers.

- How to pleat paper
- To follow directions

## Materials List

• A 20-sheet package of tissue wrapping paper, 1′6″ × 2′2″ (One package will give you enough tissue for 6 flowers)
- Scissors
- 6 rubber bands

## Directions

Cut the package of tissue paper in half across the middle without opening it or unfolding it.

Count out 6 to 8 sheets of tissue for each flower. Treat them as if they were a single sheet.

Help the children start at the narrow end of the tissue paper and fold it in 1/2-inch pleats. Make sure they press down hard to crease the folded edges.

Double a rubber band tightly around the middle of the pleated tissue (Fig. 7-6).

Show the children how to carefully separate one thin sheet of tissue paper. Tug at it gently until it is sticking up in the air. Continue pulling it upward completely around the flower (Fig. 7-7).

Each child should separate a second sheet of tissue paper and pull it upward all the way around. They should continue separating and pulling up the layers of tissue paper until all the layers are pulled up.

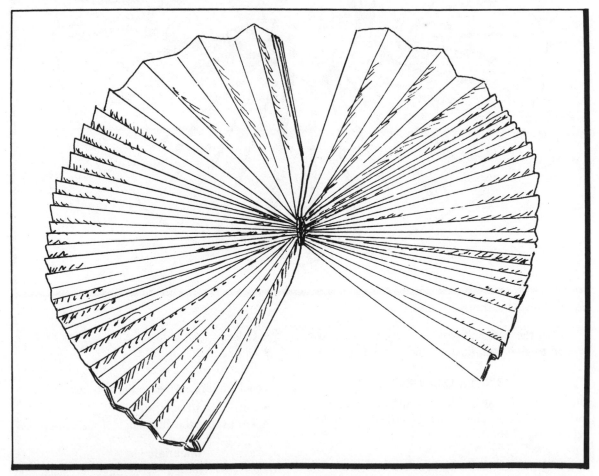

Fig. 7-6. Tissue Paper Flowers: Step 1.

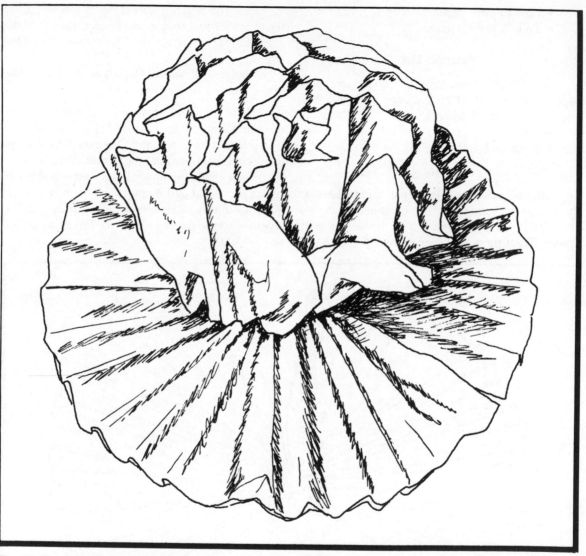

Fig. 7-7. Tissue Paper Flowers: Step 2.

Pull the bottom layer downward all the way around to give each flower a fluffy look (Fig. 7-8).

### CRAYON LEAF PRINT

On one of your walks with the children, you can let them collect leaves to use to make crayon leaf prints (Fig. 7-9).

### Skills to Teach

Teach children 2 years old and up:

- Coloring skills
- Gluing skills
- How to write his or her own name

Teach children 4 years old and up:

- Cutting skills
- To observe the different leaf shapes of trees

### Materials List

- Several fall leaves of different sizes and shapes

- Scissors
- Crayons
- Glue
- Construction paper and white paper

### Directions

Children 2 years old to 4 years old can color all over a piece of white paper, using many different colors of crayons. When a child finishes coloring a page, place a leaf that he has collected on it, and trace around the leaf with a permanent marker. He can cut out the leaf shape, or you can cut it out for him. Then he should glue these leaf shapes in a random pattern on a sheet of construction paper.

Children 4 years old and up put a leaf under a sheet of white paper. Turn the leaf upside down so the veins lay against the paper. Using only one color, rub the crayon gently back and forth on the paper until the entire leaf shows up clearly. The children can repeat this process with five or six leaves, using a different color of crayon for each. Then they can cut out the leaves and glue them in a scattered fashion on a sheet of construction paper (Fig. 7-9).

Each child should print his or her name on the front of the paper. Make sure they hold their

Fig. 7-8. Tissue Paper Flowers: Step 3.

Fig. 7-9. Crayon Leaf Prints.

crayons correctly when writing and coloring, and that they use uppercase and lowercase letters.

## TWO-PIECE PUZZLES

This craft is especially useful for very young children. Older children can make these puzzles as a gift for their younger friends (Fig. 7-10).

### Skills to Teach

Teach children 2 years old and up:

- How to put puzzles together
- The *circle, square, diamond, rectangle,* and *triangle* shapes
- How to read the names of the shapes

Fig. 7-10. 2-Piece Puzzles.

## Materials List

- 5 styrofoam meat trays
- A permanent marker
- A razor blade for you to use
- A ruler

## Directions

Wash and dry the meat trays. With a permanent marker, draw one large shape on each tray. You might use a cereal bowl or a coffee cup to draw a circle. Use the ruler to draw a square, diamond, rectangle, and triangle on the other four trays.

Use the razor blade to carefully cut the shape out of the tray, so the tray and the shape stay intact.

Print the name of each shape on the tray and on the cutout shape with the marker.

Show your children how to put the shapes back in their holes. They can learn to match and read the names of the shapes at the same time.

You can teach them the names of the five shapes by saying, "Here is a tray that says *Diamond*. Which is the *diamond* shape? Can you put it in the puzzle?" Show them the diamond shape matches the hole in the diamond tray. Also point out that it is the same as the word *Diamond* printed on the shape. Go through this process very quickly to keep their attention.

Repeat this method to teach a child the other shapes. Then try this game: give him the five shapes and spread the five trays out in front of him. Point to the circle tray. Say, "This word says *Circle*. Do you have a *circle* in your hand? Does it fit in the tray? What does the word say on your shape? It says *Circle*."

Repeat this game with the remaining trays and shapes.

## Deli Lid Necklace

We had fun experimenting with lots of different

Fig. 7-11. A Deli Lid Necklace.

disposable plastic lids by melting them in the oven. The best ones for crafts are the deli lids (Fig. 7-11).

### Skills to Teach

Teach children 2 years old and up drawing and creating skills.

Teach children 4 years old and up cutting skills.

### Materials List

• Clear plastic lids from the grocery store deli, the kind that come on potato salad.
  • Scissors
  • A paper punch
• Permanent markers in several different colors

• Old newspapers to cover the kitchen table
• Baking sheet covered with aluminum foil
• Yarn

### Directions

Preheat the oven to 325°F, and spread newspapers on the kitchen table.

Give the children the deli lids, scissors, and markers. Tell them to cut the rim from the deli lid, leaving a large circle. Encourage children 4 years old and up to do the cutting themselves. Younger children will need help from you.

They can decorate the circle with markers by

making designs, writing their names, or drawing pictures.

Use the paper punch to make a hole in the circle. Place the circles on a baking sheet covered with aluminum foil.

Bake at 325°F for 4 minutes. The circle will curl and shrink while baking, and will be fairly flat when finished.

Remove the lids from the oven, peeling them off the aluminum foil if necessary, and let them cool. The children can thread yarn through the hole to make a necklace.

## CHEESE STRAWS

Cheese straws are a delicious treat all your children will enjoy making and eating.

### Skills to Teach

Teach children 2 years old and up:

- To sit still, listen and follow directions
- How to measure, stir, roll, and bake

### Materials List

- A large bowl
- A pastry blender or 2 table knives
- A bread board and rolling pin
- A baking sheet
- A pizza cutter
- 2 1/2 cups flour
- 1 teaspoon salt
- 1 1/2 cups grated cheddar cheese
- 2/3 cup vegetable shortening
- 1/2 cup cold water

### Directions

Help the children measure the flour, salt, grated cheese, and shortening into a large bowl. They can take turns using the pastry blender to cut the shortening and cheese into small bits the size of rice grains, or use 2 table knives in a cutting motion.

Help them measure the cold water and add it to the flour mixture. Stir until all the flour is moistened. Then the children can press the dough together by hand until it forms a smooth ball.

Divide the dough among the children. They can take turns rolling their dough very thin on the bread board. Lay the rolled dough on an ungreased baking sheet. Help the children use the pizza cutter to cut it into narrow strips.

Bake in a preheated oven at 425°F for 5 to 8 minutes, until the dough turns a golden brown. Remove the Cheese Straws from the pan with a wide spatula. Break apart when cool, and store in an airtight container.

## PEANUT BUTTER/POPCORN BALLS

The children can help you make another tasty treat, the Peanut Butter/Popcorn Balls.

### Materials List

- 8 cups popped corn in a large bowl or pan
- A 1-quart saucepan and a wooden spoon
- 1/2 cup corn syrup
- 1/4 cup sugar
- 1/2 cup peanut butter
- Butter or margarine

### Directions

Measure the corn syrup and sugar into the saucepan. Cook over medium heat, stirring constantly, until the mixture comes to a boil, and the sugar is completely dissolved.

Remove the pan from the heat and stir in the peanut butter until smooth. Pour this mixture over the popped corn. Stir it until the corn is coated.

Give each child a small piece of butter or margarine. Tell them to coat their hands with it, and then shape the popcorn into balls the size of a baseball. They should squeeze the ball to make it stick together.

The yield is about 12 balls.

## PEANUT BUTTER CRUMBLES

These treats are called Crumbles because they crumble when you eat them.

### Skills to Teach

Teach children 2 years old and up:

- To sit still, listen, and follow directions

- Descriptive words such as *sticky, crisp, firmly,* and *delicious*
  - How to measure and stir
  - To count to *9*

## Materials List

- A 12-ounce package butterscotch chips
- 1 cup peanut butter
- 9 cups crispy rice cereal
- A large bowl and a wooden spoon
- A 10″ × 15″ jellyroll pan

## Directions

Measure the butterscotch chips and the peanut butter in the top of a double boiler. Melt over boiling water, stirring until smooth.

Microwave Directions: Measure the butterscotch chips and the peanut butter into a large microwave bowl. Microwave on high for 3 minutes.

Remove from the oven. Let the children stir this mixture with a wooden spoon until smooth.

Help the children measure and add 9 cups of crispy rice cereal. Count out loud with the children as they add it: "One . . . two . . . three . . . four . . . five . . . six . . . seven . . . eight . . . nine. How many cups of cereal did you add? *Nine.*"

The children can take turns stirring this mixture with the wooden spoon. One child at a time, please, unless you enjoy mopping the kitchen floor.

One or two children can grease the jelly roll pan with a pastry brush, a piece of waxed paper, or their hands.

Pour the Crumbles mixture into the prepared pan. The children can butter their hands and press the mixture *firmly* into the pan. The cookies will be very *sticky* until they are refrigerated. Refrigerate for 1 hour, then cut into 48 squares.

Note how *delicious* they taste. "Aren't these *delicious, crisp* Peanut Butter Crumbles!'"

# 8: August Crafts

School is approaching for older children, making it easier to interest preschoolers in alphabet crafts such as Letters in Yarn and Pretzel Alphabets. Fall crafts include pictures made of seeds and leaves that the children can gather in the garden or the park.

### THE NAPKIN GAME

Lunchtime is a good time to teach shapes. The children are starving and will not get up until you feed them. They don't realize that you are going to teach them first. Do you pass out napkins for their messy mouths? Do it with the Napkin Game.

Hold up a paper napkin. Say, "This is a square. What shape is it?"

The children answer, "A square."

Fold the napkin over into a triangle. Say, "Look! Now it's a triangle. What shape is it?"

The children say, "A triangle."

Open the napkin and fold it into a rectangle. Tell them, "Look! Now it's a rectangle. What shape is it?"

The children answer, "A rectangle."

Next say, "If you can tell me the shape, you can have the napkin." Fold the napkin into a triangle or a rectangle, or leave it as a square. Then call a child by name. "Mary, what shape is this?"

Mary says, "A triangle."

Tell her, "That's right. You get a triangle." Give Mary the triangle napkin and quickly go on to the next child. Keep the game fast and short. Play it every day.

### CRAFT-TRAINING SKILLS TO LEARN

August crafts introduce the children to *phonics*, or the sounds the letters make in words. They can work on letters made of yarn and pretzels, and shapes made of yarn and biscuit dough.

Craft-training skills for August include:

- How to glue, cut, draw, and color
- How to read and write his or her name
- How to read and write the names of the shapes
- How to be creative with dough

• Learning how bread is made

everywhere; so this is a good outdoor craft (Fig. 8-1).

## SEED MOSAIC

A *mosaic* is a picture made of small things of different colors, arranged to form a design. When making Seed Mosaics, the seeds usually end up

### Skills to Teach

Teach children 2 years old and up:

• Drawing skills

Fig. 8-1. A Seed Mosaic.

- How to write his or her name

Teach children 4 years old and up:

- The meaning of *mosaic*
- How to follow directions
- How to create a design with seeds

## Materials List

- Newspapers
- Construction paper 12″ × 9″
- Crayons
- At least three of the following seeds, in separate bowls:
    - —Unpopped popcorn
    - —Dried pumpkin or watermelon seeds
    - —Dried beans
    - —Dried peas
    - —Bird seed
- White glue
- Plastic food storage bags 11″×13″
- Cellophane tape
- A paper punch
- Yarn

## Directions

Tell the children to draw a design on the construction paper, using crayons. The design or picture should be large enough to cover most of the page. They can draw anything, and it will be beautiful when completed in seed mosaic.

Each child should write his or her name on the paper, using uppercase and lowercase letters. Make sure they hold their crayon correctly when writing and drawing.

Cover the kitchen table or a picnic table outside with newspapers.

Spread glue on part of each child's picture. If he has drawn a house, for instance, cover only the roof. Let him pour one kind of seed, such as popcorn, on the glue. Then he can turn the picture on end, dumping the popcorn off. Some will stick to the glue on the picture. Return the rest to its bowl.

Cover another part of each child's picture with glue. If he has drawn a scribble all over the page, follow part of the scribble with glue. Let him pour

on a second kind of seed. He can then dump it off and return it to its container. Some will remain stuck to the glue, and you will see an attractive design beginning to take shape.

Continue with the rest of the picture and the remaining seeds, until each child's entire tracing is covered in seeds of different kinds.

Let the design lay flat to dry overnight.

The next day slip the picture into a food storage bag. Fold the end of the bag over and tape it shut to keep loose seeds from falling on the floor.

Punch two holes through each paper and plastic in the top of the picture, one on each side. Tie a piece of yarn through the holes to hang up the Seed Mosaic.

If the picture bends and cannot be hung, tape a piece of heavy cardboard 2 × 12 inches on the back, just below the holes.

### TOOTHPICK PICTURE

A box of toothpicks, construction paper, and glue are all you need for these Toothpick Pictures (Fig. 8-2).

## Skills to Teach

Teach children 2 years old and up:

- The color *black*
- Eye-hand coordination
- How to use imagination to "draw" with toothpicks

## Materials List

- Black construction paper
- A box of toothpicks
- White glue

## Directions

Give your children some toothpicks and a sheet of construction paper. Tell them to make a picture or a design by arranging the toothpicks on the *black* paper.

When they are finished, glue their toothpick picture to the paper by picking the toothpicks up one by one, applying white glue, and putting them

Fig. 8-2. A Toothpick Picture.

back in their place. Children 6 years old and up can do this step themselves.

If they tell you a story about their Toothpick Picture, jot it down and glue it to the picture.

### SHAPES IN YARN

The Shapes in Yarn is another craft to help teach your children about the five basic shapes (Fig. 8-3).

### Skills to Teach

Teach children 2 years old and up:

• The 5 basic shapes: circle, square, rectangle, triangle, and diamond
• How to write the names of the shapes, using small letters
• How to read the names of the shapes

### Materials List

• Construction paper
• Yarn
• White glue in a squeeze bottle
• Crayons
• A wet cloth for sticky fingers

### Directions

Give each child five sheets of construction paper and five pieces of yarn cut in 20-inch lengths. Tell them to use a piece of yarn to make a *circle* on their paper. Then you can glue it for them.

After they have made a large circle, move the yarn out of the way and squeeze glue onto the paper in the yarn's place. Your child can help you shape the yarn into a circle again, pressing it into the glue.

Say to them, "Now let's write the word *circle* at the bottom of the page." Spell the word out loud and help them write the lowercase letters. Hold their hands lightly if necessary to help them print neatly.

Repeat with the next four shapes. As you work together to glue the yarn, talk about the shape you are gluing, such as, "This square has four sides and four corners. The sides have to be the same length. Let's pinch this yarn (or cut it) to form the four corners."

"The triangle only has three sides and three corners."

"Push the sides of the circle out to make it fat and round."

"This rectangle is shaped just like a door. It has two long sides and two short sides."

When completed, the five Shapes in Yarn can be displayed in a row so each child can feel them and read them whenever he wishes.

You might give them an extra sheet of paper and more yarn to let him create a shape of their own. They can name the shape themselves, such as "face," "cloud," or "hotdog." Then you can help them write that name on their page.

## LETTERS IN YARN

You can also use yarn and construction paper to teach the children the alphabet (Fig. 8-4).

### Skills to Teach

Teach children 2 years old and up letters of the alphabet, and the sounds they make.

### Materials List

- Construction paper
- Yarn and scissors
- White glue

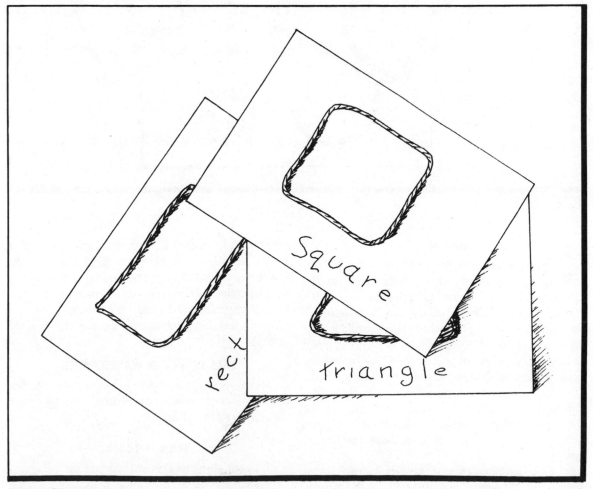

Fig. 8-3. Shapes in Yarn.

Fig. 8-4. Letters in Yarn.

### Directions

Cut each sheet of construction paper in half, making two cards per sheet. Give these to the children, along with yarn and scissors.

Help the children form the yarn into letters of the alphabet, putting both the uppercase and lowercase form of the letter on each card. They can make as many or as few letters as they like, using the scissors to snip short pieces of yarn when needed.

As the children shape the letters on the cards, carefully move the yarn over. Apply glue to the paper where the yarn was. Let the children help you press the yarn into the glue to shape the letters again.

To teach phonics with Letters in Yarn, comment, "What a good *R* you made, Ricky. Your name starts with *R*, doesn't it? Can you think of any other words that start with the *R* sound?" Help think of a few *R* words. Emphasize the beginning *R* sound by repeating the words you both think of. For instance, r-r-r-refrigerator, r-r-r-rug, r-r-r-ring. Use this teaching technique for any letters the children are making.

### FALL LEAVES IN WAXED PAPER

Go for a walk with the children, helping them gather colorful leaves. When you return, you can make them into a craft (Fig. 8-5).

### Skills to Teach

Teach children 2 years old and up:

• How to write his or her name

- That pretty fall leaves are on the ground
- Gluing skills

Teach children four years old and up:

- Cutting skills
- How to create an artistic picture from things of nature

## Materials List

- A place to gather fall leaves
- A padded ironing board
- An iron
- Newspaper
- Waxed paper
- Construction paper
- A pencil
- Glue

## Directions

The children should gather three or four leaves each. Choose ones that are fairly flat and not too dry. Bring them home.

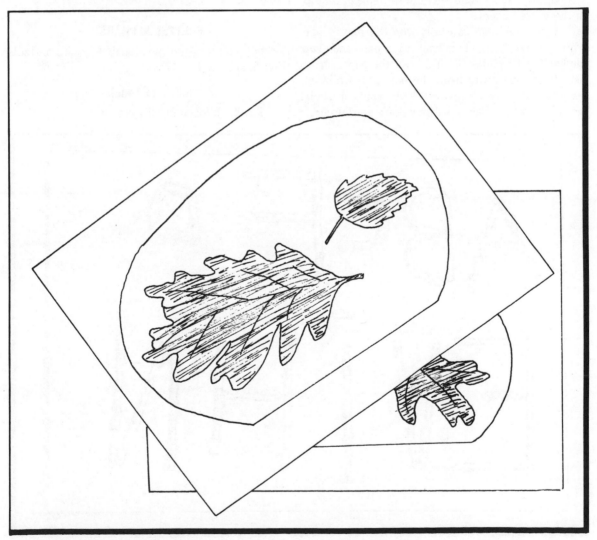

Fig. 8-5. Fall Leaves in Waxed Paper.

Adjust the ironing board so it's at a height the children can reach easily. Turn the temperature gauge to "low" on a dry iron. Put two layers of newspaper on the ironing board.

Tear off a strip of waxed paper 16 inches long for each child. Fold it in half like a book and place it on the newspaper layers. Open the waxed paper "book" and let each child arrange his or her leaves on half of it, single layer, Help the child fold the "book" shut again so the leaves are sandwiched in the waxed paper.

Gently lay a single sheet of newspaper on top of the waxed paper.

Each child can carefully iron the newspaper while you hold both of his hands: Put one hand over his hand as he glides the iron over the paper; hold his other hand away from the hot iron. Children automatically try to involve both hands in their work. Hold both hands so they don't get burned.

Lift the top newspaper. Gently remove the waxed paper with the leaves sealed inside. Let it cool a few minutes.

Give each child scissors, glue, a sheet of construction paper, and a pencil. They should trim off some of the excess waxed paper and use glue to mount their sealed leaves on the construction paper.

Help each child write his or her name on the front of the picture. Make sure they use uppercase and lowercase letters and that they hold their pencils properly.

### PRETZEL ALPHABET

Another way to teach the alphabet is with pretzels (Fig. 8-6).

### Skills to Teach

Teach children of all ages:

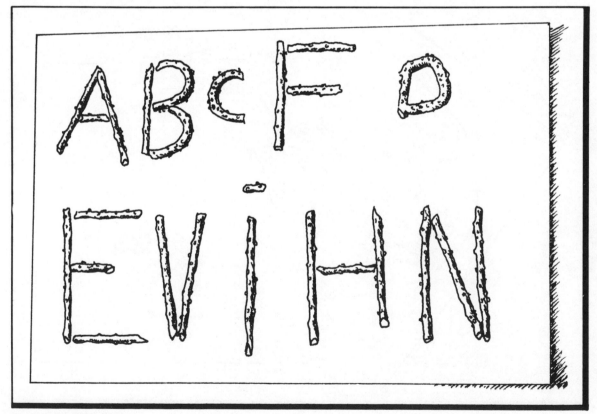

Fig. 8-6. Pretzel Alphabet.

- How to form letters of the alphabet
- How to write his or her first and last name

## Materials List

- A sheet of construction paper for each child
- A pencil for each child
- A box of straight pretzel sticks
- A box of twisted pretzels
- White glue

## Directions

Give each of the children a sheet of construction paper and a pencil. Help them print their first and last names on the paper. Make sure each one holds the pencil the right way. Spell the children's names out loud to them as they write the letters. "Your last name is Smith. *S—M—I—T—H*."

Put a bowl of straight pretzels and a bowl of twisted pretzels on the table where everyone can reach them. It's best to do this craft after lunch when they're not too hungry.

Show them how to make letters by putting the pretzels together on their sheet of construction paper, breaking them when needed. The children will come up with some pretty interesting combinations.

When they have finished, they can glue the letters they have made to the construction paper for display and eat the scraps.

## BAKE-A-SHAPE

The five basic shapes are the basis for the Bake-A-Shape project. One shape can be taught per session.

## Skills to Teach

Teach children 2 years old and up:

- The 5 basic shapes: *rectangle, square, circle, triangle,* and *diamond*
- How to work with dough
- To sit still, listen, and follow directions
- How to write his or her name

## Materials List

- A can of refrigerator biscuits. (Plan on using

three biscuits per child.)
- Melted butter and a pastry brush
- 1/4 cup sugar mixed with 1 tablespoon cinnamon
- A baking sheet covered with aluminum foil
- Paper plates
- Markers or crayons

## Directions

Give each child three refrigerator biscuits. Tell them to roll each biscuit into a long snake.

They can take turns placing their snakes on the foil-covered baking sheet, pinching them together to form a shape, such as a *rectangle*.

Then they can brush the shape with melted butter and sprinkle it with the cinnamon-sugar mixture.

Bake in a preheated oven at 475° F for 4 or 5 minutes.

While the shapes are baking, give each of the children a paper plate and markers or crayons. Tell them to turn their plates over and to print their names, using uppercase and lowercase letters, on the back of the plate. Make sure they hold the markers correctly when writing.

Carefully transfer the cooled shapes to the children's plates. Ask each child the name of the shape he has baked, or comment," You certainly did a good job baking that *rectangle*."

Repeat this activity at another time to teach a different shape.

## COFFEE CAN COOKIE JAR

Do this project one day and a cookie project the next, so each child can have his or her own cookies in a cookie jar (Fig. 8-7).

## Skills to Teach

Teach children 2 years old and up:

- Drawing, coloring, and gluing skills
- How to write his or her name

Teach children 4 years old and up cutting skills.

## Materials List

- A ruler and pencil

Fig. 8-7. A Coffee Can Cookie Jar.

cans with paper themselves. Children 6 and 7 years old can glue the paper if you measure and cut it for them. Younger children should be given the covered can to decorate.

Lay the remaining scrap of construction paper on the plastic lid. Run a pencil around the inside circle of the lid to mark the paper. Cut out this circle and glue it on the lid.

Give your children the white paper, markers, crayons, scissors, and glue. Tell them to draw and color lots of cookies of different shapes and sizes. Then they can cut them out and glue them all over their cookie jar.

Each child should print his or her name, using uppercase and lowercase letters, on the paper-covered lid.

Fill the jar with cookies that they have helped make.

### OATMEAL MIX-IT-UP COOKIES

Oatmeal Mix-It-Up Cookies are delicious treats that can be put in the children's cookie jars.

### Skills to Teach

Teach children 2 years old and up:

- How to work with dough
- How to read names
- To become familiar with their own last name

### Materials List

- A large bowl and a wooden spoon
- 1 cup flour
- 2 cups quick-cooking oatmeal
- 1 cup brown sugar
- 1 cup margarine (2 sticks) at room temperature
- 1 teaspoon baking soda
- A small drinking glass
- A cereal bowl 1/2 full of sugar

### Directions

Put aprons on everyone and gather them around the kitchen table.

The children can measure the flour, oatmeal,

- Scissors
- A 13-ounce coffee can with a plastic lid for each child
- Construction paper
- White glue
- Cellophane tape
- White (typing) paper
- Water-based markers and crayons

### Directions

Using a ruler, pencil, and scissors, cut a strip of construction paper 5 1/2 × 12 inches for each cookie jar. This strip will not fit all the way around the coffee cans, so cut a second piece of construction paper 5 1/2 × 3 1/2 inches for each can.

Apply the smaller piece of paper to the can first. Spread glue on it and press it onto the can just under the top metal rim. Tuck the excess paper under the can.

Apply the larger piece of paper in the same way. Tape the seams and bottom to hold the paper securely.

Children 8 years old and up can cover their

brown sugar, margarine, and baking soda into the large bowl.

They can mix the dough by squeezing it with their hands until it is blended, or by using the wooden spoon.

Then they can pinch off pieces of dough, rolling them into 1-inch balls and placing them on an ungreased cookie sheet.

Next they should press each cookie flat, but not too flat, with the bottom of the small glass dipped in sugar.

When all cookies have been flattened, bake in a preheated 350° F oven for 10 minutes.

While the cookies are baking, print the children's first and last names on a paper plate, one for each child. Use uppercase and lowercase letters. Then hold up a plate so the children can see the name. Ask, "Whose plate is this? If this is your name, raise your hand." This a good game even if you are working with only one child. Seeing his first and last name helps him grow accustomed to how it looks and to the letters that are in it. It also teaches him his last name, if he doesn't already know it.

When the cookies are baked, let each child take his share from the baking sheet with a spatula, putting the cookies on his own paper plate.

## BAKING BREAD

Bread-baking is a traditional activity that children love. Homemade bread smells great, tastes great, and even the youngest child can turn the dough into an imaginative shape.

### Skills to Teach

Teach children 2 years old and up:

- To sit still, listen, and follow directions
- How to measure, stir, and bake
- To be creative with dough
- How bread is made

### Materials List

- A large bowl and a wooden spoon
- One or two greased baking sheets
- 2 1/4 cups lukewarm water
- 2 packages active dry yeast
- 7 1/4 cups flour, divided into 2 piles
- 3 tablespoons sugar
- 1 tablespoon salt
- 2 tablespoons vegetable shortening

### Directions

Help the children measure the lukewarm water into the bowl. They can stir in the yeast, 1/2 of the flour, the sugar, salt, and vegetable shortening. Let them take turns stirring this mixture until it is smooth.

Add and mix in the rest of the flour to make a stiff dough. Put the dough on a tabletop or breadboard with a little extra flour to keep it from sticking. Knead it by folding it over and pressing down hard with the heel of your hand. Keep kneading it for 10 minutes, until it forms a smooth elastic ball. The children will love to help you if you get tired.

Grease a large bowl with shortening. Put the dough in the bowl. Turn the dough upside down to grease its top. Cover the bowl with plastic wrap to keep the dough from drying out, and set it in a warm place for 1 1/2 hours.

Punch the dough down with your fingers and turn it over. Cover it again and let it rise for 30 minutes.

Put aprons on the children and seat them around the kitchen table. Give each child a small pile of flour that they can spread around in front of them. Tell them not to clap their hands.

Give each child a portion of dough. They can play with it as long as they wish; lots of kneading only makes better bread. When they tire of playing with the dough they can shape it in many ways, such as a round loaf, a long loaf, a baseball and bat, a dough boy, a basket with eggs, a bird's nest with eggs, or whatever.

They can place their creations on the greased baking sheets. Let them rise for 1 hour.

Bake in a preheated oven at 425°F for 20 minutes, or until the bread is a rich golden brown. As soon as the bread comes out of the oven, brush it with soft shortening or butter for a soft, glowing crust.

# 9: September Crafts

In this chapter the children are repeatedly exposed to shapes, letters, phonics, and numbers in a concentrated collection of learning crafts. Projects include several shapes, pictures, alphabet games to make and bake, and egg-carton counting games.

### MORE TEACH 'N TRAVEL

We can teach colors to children all day. With the number of traffic lights that stop us when we drive, our children should know the colors *red* and *green* by the age of 2. Yellow traffic lights aren't very useful for teaching, however, because they stay on such a short time. Besides, sometimes they are orange.

To teach red and green, however, each time you pull up to a red light, say, "Look! A red light! We have to stop." Children will learn readily this way. When the light turns green, say, "Green light! Now we can go."

Remember that the children in your car cannot escape your teaching. They are the classic "captive audience." You can teach them numbers by pointing out signs along the road. Say, "Look! That sign says

*35.*" The next time you see one, say, "Liz, there's another sign with a *3* and a *5*. What number is that?" If Liz doesn't know it's a *35*, tell her. Then ask immediately, "What number was that? 35. That's right, Liz."

### CRAFT-TRAINING SKILLS TO LEARN

The children will feel like they are going to school with their older friends by the time they finish this chapter. September Craft-training skills include:

• Matching uppercase and lowercase letters of the alphabet

• Learning phonics with a sound box

• Counting and reading numbers

• Learning the meaning of *left, right, above, behind,* and *extends*

• Learning to write his or her first and last name

• Learning to write other words like *School Bus* and *Truck*

• Plenty of practice in drawing, cutting, and gluing

• Learning the names of the colors and shapes

## APPLE TREE AND HOUSE PICTURE

This first September project teaches both colors and shapes, and many other skills, as well (Fig. 9-1).

### Skills to Teach

Teach children 2 years old and up:

• The colors *blue, brown, red, green,* and *yellow*

• The *rectangle, square, circle,* and *triangle* shapes

• To count to *6*
• Drawing skills
• Gluing skills
• How to write his or her first and last name

Teach children 4 years old and up:

• Cutting skills
• The meaning of *left, right,* and *above*

### Materials List

• Construction paper in the following colors: light blue, dark blue, brown, red, green, and yellow
• A ruler and a pencil
• Crayons or narrow-tipped markers
• Scissors
• Glue

### Directions

For each picture, use the pencil and ruler to draw a brown rectangle 1 × 3 inches, a red rectangle 1 × 1 1/2 inches, and a dark square 4 × 4 inches. Use the pattern to trace a brown triangle roof, a green circle tree, a yellow circle sun, and six small red circles for apples (Fig. 9-2). Repeat this step for each child.

Cut these shapes out for younger children. Encourage children 4 years old and up to cut out the shapes after you have drawn them.

Each child should have a set of shapes and a sheet of light blue paper on which to glue them.

Fig. 9-1. The Apple Tree and House Picture.

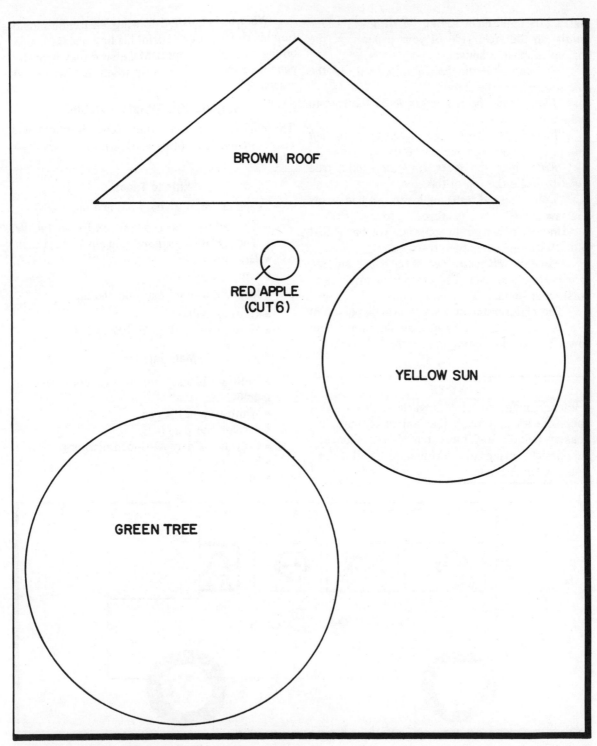

Fig. 9-2. The patterns for the Apple Tree and House Picture.

Instruct the children by saying, *"First,* glue the *blue square* on the *right* side of your paper near the bottom to make a house.

*"Second,* glue the *brown triangle above* the *blue square* to make a roof.

*"Third,* glue the *red rectangle* on the roof to make a chimney.

*"Fourth,* glue the *brown rectangle* on the *left* side of the paper to make a tree trunk.

*"Fifth,* glue the *green circle above* the tree trunk to make the top of the tree.

*"Count the *red circle* apples to see how many you have. One . . . two . . . three . . . four . . . five . . . six. How many red circle apples do you have? *Six!* Glue these onto the apple tree.

*"Glue the *yellow circle above* the house and tree to make the sun. Now use crayons or markers to finish your picture."

The children might want to draw a person to live in the house. They can draw doors and windows, and smoke coming out of the chimney.

---

### NOTE

Before giving your child a whole apple, push a popsicle stick through the bottom to make it easier to hold and more fun to eat. Chinese chopsticks make wonderful long handles for Apples-On-A-Stick.

---

When he is finished drawing, each child should turn his paper over and print his first and last name on the back of the paper. Make sure they hold the pencils or markers correctly when they write and draw.

## SCHOOL BUS SHAPES PICTURE

The children can draw their older brothers and sisters in this School Bus, and learn while they draw (Fig. 8-3).

### Skills to Teach

Teach children 2 years old and up:

- The colors *yellow, black, orange,* and *white*
- The *rectangle, square,* and *circle* shapes
- Drawing skills
- Gluing skills

Teach children 4 years old and up:

- Cutting skills
- How to write the word *School Bus*

### Materials List

- Yellow, black, and orange construction paper
- White (typing) paper
- A ruler and pencil
- Crayons or narrow-tipped markers
- Scissors
- Glue

Fig. 9-3. The School Bus Shapes Picture.

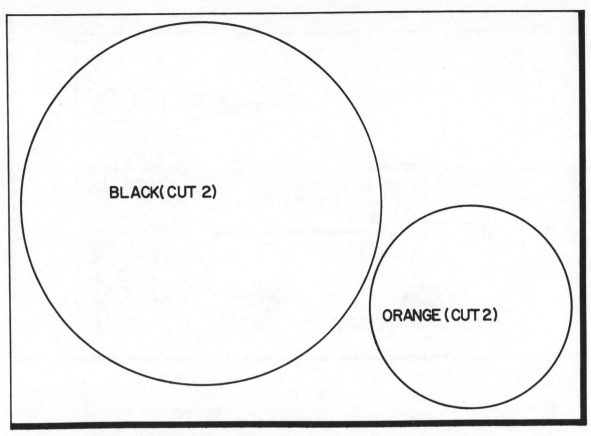

BLACK(CUT 2)

ORANGE (CUT 2)

Fig. 9-4. The patterns to make the School Bus Shapes Picture.

### Directions

For each picture, use a pencil and ruler to draw a yellow rectangle 8 × 12 inches, a yellow square 4 × 4 inches, and three white rectangles 2 × 3 inches. Use the pattern in Fig. 9-4 to trace two large black circles and two smaller orange circles.

Cut these shapes out. Encourage children 4 years old and up to cut their own shapes after you have drawn them.

Give each child a set of shapes. Instruct the children by saying, "To make a bus, glue the *yellow square* onto the end of the *yellow rectangle*.

"Glue the *2 large black circles* on the bus to make tires. Glue the *small orange circles* on top of the black tires to make hubcaps.

"Draw a boy or girl on the *3 white rectangles*. Glue them on the bus to make windows with children looking out.

"Now use your crayons or markers to draw a driver for the bus. Print the words *School Bus* on the side of the bus.

### TRUCK SHAPES PICTURE

Children are fascinated by trucks of all kinds. They'll enjoy making a picture of trucks, and they'll learn shapes, too (Fig. 9-5).

### Skills to Teach

Teach children 2 years old and up:

- The colors *red, black, brown,* and *blue*
- The *rectangle, square, circle,* and *triangle* shapes
- Drawing skills
- Gluing skills

Teach children 4 years old and up:

131

Fig. 9-5. The Truck Shapes Picture.

- Cutting skills
- How to write the word *truck*
- The meaning of many words such as *left, right, narrow, extends,* and *behind*

### Materials List

- Red, black, brown, and blue construction paper
  - A ruler and pencil
  - Scissors
  - Glue
  - Crayons or narrow-tipped markers

### Directions

For each picture, use the pencil and ruler to draw a brown rectangle 3 × 8 inches, a skinny brown rectangle 1/4 × 8 inches, a red rectangle 4 × 6 inches, and a red square 2 × 2 inches. Use the pattern to trace a black triangle roof and two black circle wheels (Fig. 9-6).

Cut these shapes out for younger children. Encourage children 4 years old and up to do their own cutting after you draw the shapes for them.

Give each child a set of shapes and a sheet of blue construction paper on which to assemble the picture. Instruct the children by saying: "*First,* glue the *large brown rectangle* on the *right* side of the *blue* paper to make a tall building.

"*Second,* glue the *red rectangle* next to the tall building. Glue the *red square* on the *left* side of the red rectangle to make a truck.

"*Third,* glue *two black circle* tires to the bottom of the truck. Glue the skinny *brown rectangle* below the tires to make a road.

"*Fourth,* print the word *Truck* on the side of the truck.

"*Fifth,* glue the *black triangle* roof on the side of the building so that it *extends over* the truck. Now use crayons or markers to finish your picture. You might draw a person driving the truck with engine exhaust coming from *behind* it. You can add windows to the building, too."

Fig. 9-6. The patterns for the roof and wheels of the Truck Shapes Picture.

### PAPER SAUCER FACE

Shown in Fig. 9-7, the Paper Saucer Face is a delightful project to do with your children.

### Skills to Teach

Teach children 2 years old and up:

- The colors *brown, black, blue, red,* and *pink*
- Gluing skills
- The *circle* and *rectangle* shapes

Teach children 5 years old and up:

- Cutting skills

Fig. 9-7. The Paper Saucer Face.

- The meaning of many words such as *larger* and *smaller*, *first*, *second*, and *third*

## Materials List

- 6″ paper saucers, plain white
- Brown, black, blue, red, and pink construction paper
- A pencil and ruler
- Scissors
- Glue

## Directions

For each face, use the pencil and ruler to draw two brown rectangles 1 1/2 × 6 inches and a brown rectangle 2 × 4 inches. Trace the pattern in Fig. 9-8 to make two blue circle eyes, two black circle eyeballs, two pink cheeks, a pink circle nose, and a red mouth.

Cut the shapes out for younger children. Encourage children 5 years old and up to cut their own after you have drawn them.

Give each child the cutout pieces, a paper saucer, and glue. Then tell them the following: "*First, fringe* the two *larger brown rectangles* the long way to make hair. Curl the hair by wrapping the fringes tightly around a pencil.

"*Second,* fringe the *smaller brown rectangle* the short way, curling it around a pencil to form bangs. Glue the brown hair and bangs onto the paper saucer.

"*Third,* glue on the *blue circle* eyes. Glue the *black circle* eyeballs on the blue eyes.

"*Fourth,* glue the *red* mouth on the Paper Saucer Face. Add the *two pink circle* cheeks and the *pink circle* nose.

"*Fifth,* use crayons to draw on eyelashes and eyebrows."

## BISCUIT ALPHABET

Just as you used biscuits to teach shapes, you can also use them to teach the alphabet and the sounds the letters make.

### Skills to Teach

Teach children 2 years old and up the letters of the alphabet and the sounds they make.

### Materials List

- A baking sheet or two, coated with vegetable cooking spray
- Refrigerator biscuits. (Plan on using three biscuits per child.)
- 1/4 cup melted butter or margarine
- 1/2 cup sugar mixed with 2 tablespoons cinnamon

### Directions

Give each child three refrigerator biscuits. Tell them to roll each biscuit into a long snake.

Fig. 9-8. The patterns to make the Paper Saucer Face.

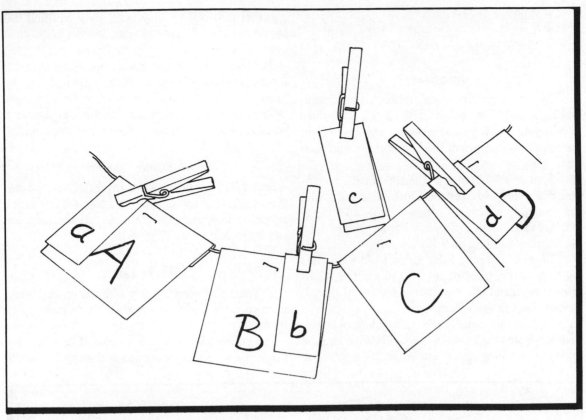

Fig. 9-9. The Alphabet Clothesline.

They can take turns dipping their biscuits in the melted butter. Then they should coat their biscuits with the cinnamon-sugar mixture.

Help the children place their biscuits on the baking sheet, arranging and pinching them together to form letters. They could make a letter that you are trying to teach that day, a letter the child is having trouble learning, or the first letter in the child's name.

To teach phonics with Biscuit Alphabets, comment, "I like the *M* you're making, Mary. How does the *M* sound? It sounds like this, doesn't it? M-m-m-m. Can you think of some words that start with the *M* sound?" Help her think of a few *M* words. Emphasize the beginning *M* sound by repeating the words you both think of. For instance, M-m-m-mary, m-m-m-mommy, m-m-m-mouse.

Bake in a preheated oven at 400°F for 10 minutes. Take the letters off the baking sheet im-mediately and let them cool on a cooling rack or a piece of foil.

## ALPHABET CLOTHESLINE

The Alphabet Clothesline is a great tool to teach children about uppercase and lowercase letters.

### Skills to Teach

Teach children 2 years old and up to match the uppercase and lowercase letters of the alphabet.

### Materials List

- 2 chairs
- A piece of string or rope 8′ long. (You can use anything from clothesline to kite string.)
- Typing paper
- Construction paper
- Scissors

- Markers or crayons
- A stapler
- 26 clip clothespins

### Directions

Tie the rope or string between two chairs, making it taut. Cut 26 rectangles 3 1/2 × 4 inches from typing paper. Use a marker or crayons to print the uppercase letters of the alphabet, one on each rectangle.

Fold down 1/2 inch at the top of each rectangle. Place this fold over the Clothesline and staple the rectangle in place. Do this with all 26 letters, stapling them up in alphabetical order so they look like clothes hanging on a line.

Now cut 26 rectangular strips 1 1/2 × 6 inches from construction paper. Fold each in half crosswise. Print the lowercase letters of the alphabet, one on each strip.

To play this game, each child picks any lowercase letter and hunts along the Clothesline until he finds the matching uppercase letter. If they say the alphabet out loud as they hunt, they will find the letters faster. They will also learn alphabetical order as they play.

Then they clip the lowercase letter over its partner with a clothespin. A child can play this game alone, but the spirit of competition makes playing it with a friend or two more fun. He can also play with an adult who has suddenly developed amnesia.

## A SOUND BOX

A Sound Box can be made for any letter or combination of letters in the alphabet. Its purpose is to teach children the sound a letter makes (phonics) in a fun and interesting way (Fig. 9-10).

### Skills to Teach

Teach children 2 years old and up beginning phonics, or how a letter sounds at the beginning of a word.

Teach children 6 years old and up advanced phonics—how a letter sounds at the end of a word,

Fig. 9-10. A Sound Box.

Fig. 9-11. The Popsicle Stick Counting project.

or consonant blends such as *th*, *ch*, and *sh* at the beginning or end of a word.

### Materials List

- An empty cardboard box, such as a large shoe box
  - Construction paper
  - Markers
  - Glue

### Directions

Select a letter that you want to teach the children. The letter *M* is a good one to do first.

Use the markers to print both the uppercase and lowercase form of the letter on construction paper. Glue the paper to the front of the cardboard box.

Tell the children, "This is the letter *M*. What letter is it?"

The children say, "*M*."

Then say, "The letter *M* sounds like this, m-m-m-m. Can you think of anything that starts with the *M* sound?"

If the children can't, give them some exam-ples. "How about m-m-m-marker?" Put the marker in the Sound Box. "Let's all say m-m-m-marker."

The children respond, "M-m-m-marker."

Then say, "Let's look around the playroom and find more things that start with the *M* sound." Walk slowly around the room, saying m-m-m as if to yourself, but loud enough for everyone to hear you. Soon the children will be making the *M* sound, too.

Help them find about 10 items that start with *M*, and put them in the Sound Box. Then pull out each item and say its name, heavily emphasizing the *M* sound.

See if the children can take turns saying the names of the items just as you did.

Leave the Box in a place where the children can play with the *M* toys.

After about three days, take off the construction paper *M* page, and repeat this game with a new sound, such as *S*.

### POPSICLE STICK COUNTING

This project can be used many times to teach your children to count (Fig. 9-11).

Teach children 2 years old and up:

- How to read numbers from 1 to 6
- How to put these numbers in the right order
- To count each number from 1 to 6

### Materials List

- 6 6-oz. frozen orange juice cans with the top removed
  - Construction paper
  - Ruler and pencil
  - Scissors
  - Glue
  - Transparent tape
  - Black marker
  - 21 popsicle sticks

### Directions

Rinse and dry the six orange juice cans. Use the ruler and pencil to measure six rectangles 3 3/4 × 7 1/2 inches from construction paper. Cut them out.

Spread glue on the rectangles and wrap each one neatly around an orange juice can, covering it completely. Tape the seam to make sure it is secure.

Use the black marker to write a 2-inch-high number on each can, from 1 to 6.

Give your children the orange juice cans. Help each one read the number on each can by saying, "Terry, this is the number 1. What number is it?" Tell them what the number is until they can tell you.

Help them put the cans in numerical order. Read the numbers out loud with them.

Now give them 21 clean popsicle sticks. Dirty ones stick together and are hard to count. Show them how to count one stick, putting it in can number 1, count two sticks, putting them in can number 2, and so on until the six cans are filled with the correct number of sticks.

Be sure to reward them for doing all that counting.

### EGG CARTON COUNTING

It's important for children to learn to count, but they soon tire of one method. Here's another project you can use to keep their interest (Fig. 9-12).

### Skills to Teach

Teach children 2 years old and up:

- How many make each number from *1* to *12*
- Lots of counting
- What is a *dozen*
- How to read numbers from left to right

### Materials List

- A styrofoam egg carton
- A sheet of construction paper
- Scissors
- Glue
- A pen or fine-tipped marker
- A box of toothpicks or raisins

### Directions

Cut 12 circles the size of a dime from construction paper. Write one number on each circle, 1 through 12.

Glue the circles in order in the bottom of the egg cups, going left to right, as shown in Fig. 9-12.

Give your child 78 toothpicks. To play the game he should read the number *1*, then place one toothpick in the egg cup. Then he should read number *2* and place two toothpicks in that egg cup, and so on until each cup is filled with the correct number of toothpicks. One child can play this game while another plays the Popsicle Stick Counting Game.

Counting 78 toothpicks takes a lot of time and patience. Let your child work this game as long as he is interested. Reward him or her (with a kiss for being a smart boy or girl?) for completing even part of it.

### EGG CARTON NUMBERS

You can make two games for the Egg Carton, one more advanced than the other. The first game involves simply matching numerals. The second one requires a lot of counting. Both games introduce the child to number words (Fig. 9-13).

Fig. 9-12. The Egg Carton Counting project.

### Skills to Teach

Teach children 2 years old and up:

- What is a *dozen*
- To count to *12*
- How to match numbers
- How to put numbers in the right order (numerical sequence)

Teach children 4 years old and up:

- An introduction to number words *one* through *twelve*
- Phonics
- How to read numbers from left to right

### Materials List

- A styrofoam egg carton
- 2 sheets of construction paper of different colors
- Scissors
- Permanent marker. (A fine-tipped laundry marker works best.)

### Directions

Write the numerals 1 through 12 in the bottoms of the egg cups, going left to right, as shown in Fig. 9-13).

Fig. 9-13. Egg Carton Numbers.

Cut 12 circles the size of a 50¢ piece from each sheet of construction paper. Use 12 circles of one color for the first game, and 12 circles of a different color for the second game.

For the first and easier game, write one numeral on each circle, 1 through 12. Draw a heavy line under the numerals so the child will know which way to hold them. On the other side of the circle print the number word that corresponds to the numeral. For example, write *12* on one side of a circle, and *twelve* on the other side.

To play the game, the children should match the circles with the numerals inside the egg cups by placing the circle in the appropriate cup.

For the second game, print the number word on one side of the circle. On the other side of the circle draw neat domino dots that correspond to the number word. For example, print *six* on one side of a circle, and ::: on the other side.

To play this game, the children should look at the number word and use phonics to guess what it says. Then they can count the dots on the other side of the circle before placing it in the correct egg cup.

Show them how to use phonics to guess the number word by saying to them, "Look at the number word. What letter does it start with? It starts with an *S*. How does the *S* sound? It sounds like this: s-s-s-s. What numbers begin with the s-s-s-s sound? (Six and seven do.) Turn the circle over. Count the dots to see what the word is."

Don't force them to play this game if they become bored with it. Show them how to do it and be available if they want help.

Remember that bribery can accomplish wonderful things. Offer them a new sticker, a box of raisins, or a few jelly beans to encourage them to finish the game.

## GRANDMA'S PEANUT BUTTER COOKIES

Peanut Butter Cookies are a favorite of children. You can use them to teach, as well as to treat.

### Skills to Teach

Teach children 2 years old and up:

- To sit still, listen, and follow directions
- How to measure, stir, and bake
- How to work with dough
- How to read his or her name

### Materials List

- 1 cup margarine or butter
- 1 1/4 cups brown sugar
- 1 1/4 cups white sugar
- 2 eggs
- 1 cup peanut butter
- 1 1/4 teaspoons vanilla extract
- 2 1/2 cups flour
- 2 teaspoons baking powder
- 1 1/4 teaspoons baking soda
- 1/4 teaspoon salt
- A large bowl and a wooden spoon
- A cookie sheet
- A fork and a little bowl of flour
- Paper plates and a marker

### Directions

Help the children measure the butter, the brown sugar, and the white granulated sugar into a large bowl. They should take turns stirring with a wooden spoon until they are blended.

The children can crack the two eggs into a saucer, then add them to the dough. Stir again until blended.

Help them measure the peanut butter and vanilla, adding it to the bowl. Stir well.

Help the children measure the flour, baking powder, baking soda, and salt, and add it to the dough. They can take turns stirring again until the dough is smooth. Refrigerate the dough for 30 minutes.

While the dough is chilling, play the Read-Your-Name Game. (See Chapter 11.)

After the dough is chilled, put a portion on each child's plate. They can pinch off pieces the size of a walnut, roll them into balls, and place them on an ungreased cookie sheet.

Show the children how to flatten each cookie slightly with a fork dipped in a little bowl of flour so it won't stick to the dough. They should press each cookie twice, making a crisscross design.

Bake in a preheated oven at 400°F for about 10 minutes, or until light brown around the edges.

Give each child the spatula and let him transfer his own cookies to his plate to eat or share.

# 10: October Crafts

Halloween crafts occupy the entire month while the children practice following directions, eye-hand coordination, counting skills, and recognition of shapes and colors. Three spooky recipes are included, for making Spider Bread, Witches Fingers, and Witches Bones.

### CHILDREN ARE CREATIVE

Children love to make things, and they don't have the reservations about experimenting that we adults do. If the product turns out a little odd looking, their attitude is, "So what?" The process of making it was fun, and they're willing to try again. Next time the product will probably turn out better.

Once you work on crafts with your children, they will want to create by themselves. Establish rules so the mess will be less for you. Make sure they paint or glue only in the kitchen with newspapers under their work. They would rather make crafts in the middle of their bed or on your coffee table; so you must be strict. Make sure they clean up their own messes unless you have a live-in maid.

Then make craft materials available to them. Scissors, school glue, paper, crayons, and markers can be kept in a box under your watchful eye. You can loan it out when asked. Your children may become so enthusiastic about creating things that they will give up television for a change.

### CRAFT-TRAINING SKILLS TO LEARN

October crafts introduce the children to the idea of alphabetical order as they follow step A, step B, step C, etc. They learn how to use paper fasteners, and how to fringe and pleat.

Other Craft-training skills to practice include:

- Learning to recognize colors and shapes
- Learning the meaning of *large, medium, small, tall, short, next to,* and *unfold*
- Putting things together
- Writing his or her name
- Drawing a face
- Counting to 10
- Gluing, drawing, and cutting skills

## BLACK CAT

The Black Cat is the first October craft (Fig. 10-1). You don't need many items, but the children will still enjoy making it.

### Skills to Teach

Teach children 2 years old and up:

- The *triangle, rectangle*, and *diamond* shapes
- The colors *black, green,* and *orange*
- Gluing skills

Teach children 4 years old and up:

- Cutting skills
- Assembling skills: putting things together

### Materials List

- Black, green, and orange construction paper

Fig. 10-1. The Black Cat.

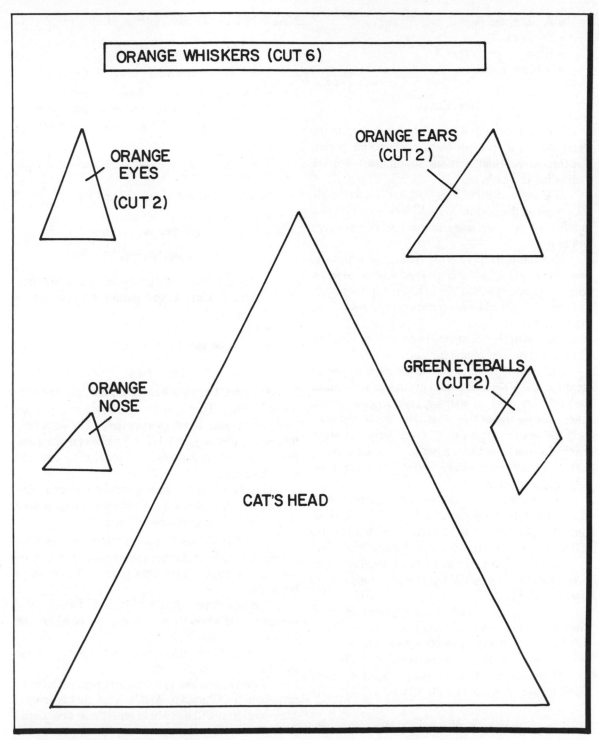

ORANGE WHISKERS (CUT 6)

ORANGE
EYES

(CUT 2)

ORANGE EARS
(CUT 2)

GREEN EYEBALLS
(CUT 2)

ORANGE
NOSE

CAT'S HEAD

Fig. 10-2. The patterns for the Black Cat.

145

- A ruler and pencil
- Scissors
- Glue
- A black marker

### Directions

For each cat, cut a strip 1 × 9 inches from the short side of a sheet of black construction paper. Cut this strip in half, forming two strips 1 × 4 1/2 inches for the cat's neck.

Use the pattern in Fig. 10-2 to draw a triangle cat's head on the bottom of each black rectangle that is left. Cut out the triangle, leaving the cat's legs and body.

Use the pattern to draw six orange whiskers, two orange eyes, two orange ears, an orange nose, and two green eyeballs (Fig. 10-2). Cut them out. Children 4 years old and up can cut their own if you draw them first.

Cut a strip 1 × 9 inches from another sheet of black construction paper for each cat's tail.

Making the neck is a little complex for young children, but it's a nice technique to learn. To make the neck, lay the two strips at right angles to each other, one on top of the other to form the letter *L*. Fold the bottom strip over the top strip and press down. Repeat, folding the strips upon each other until they are completely folded together. Glue both ends together.

When the neck is finished, tell each child to glue it to the *upper left corner* of the body. Help them glue the *black triangle* head to the neck, with the tip of the triangle pointing down, as shown in Fig. 10-1.

Tell them to fold the *black rectangle* tail into 1-inch pleats. They should glue it to the *upper right corner* of the body.

Next they should add the *orange triangle* ears. They can color them with the black marker. They should add the *orange triangle* eyes and nose. Then they can glue on the *green diamond* eyeballs.

Their Black Cat is finished when they have glued on six *orange rectangle* whiskers.

### DANCING PUMPKIN MAN

Children will be delighted by the Dancing Pumpkin Man, which really dances (Fig. 10-3).

### Skills to Teach

Teach children 2 years old and up:

- The colors *orange, black,* and *green*
- The *triangle, circle,* and *rectangle* shapes
- The meaning of *large, medium,* and *small*
- To count to *4*
- Gluing skills
- Drawing skills

Teach children 4 years old and up:

- Cutting skills
- How to use paper fasteners

### Materials List

- Orange, black, and green construction paper
- A black water-based marker, narrow-tipped
- Scissors
- Glue
- 5 spread-apart paper fasteners

### Directions

For each Dancing Pumpkin Man, use the patterns in Figs. 10-4 and 10-5 to draw one orange body, one orange head, two orange jack-o'-lanterns, four orange rectangles 1 1/2 × 3 inches for arms and legs, 1 green rectangle 1/2 × 1 inch for a stem, and two black feet.

Cut them out for your younger children. Encourage children 4 years old and up to cut their own shapes after you have traced them.

Give the shapes to the children, along with a black marker. Instruct them by saying, *"First,* draw lines on the *large orange circle* to make it look like a pumpkin.

*"Second,* draw a jack-o'-lantern face on the *medium-sized orange circle* to make a head for the Dancing Pumpkin Man.

*"Third,* draw jack-o'-lantern faces on the *two small orange circles.*

*"Fourth,* use the spread-apart paper fasteners to attach the Pumpkin Man's head to his body." Many children will need help with these fasteners.

"How many *orange rectangles* do you have? Let's count them together and see." Count out loud

Fig. 10-3. The Dancing Pumpkin Man.

with the children. "One... two... three... four. How many orange rectangles do you have? *Four.*" Help the children fasten the four orange rectangles to the Pumpkin Man's body to make arms and legs. Use the paper fasteners as shown in Fig. 10-3.

"Glue the *small green rectangle* to the top of the

Pumpkin Man's head for a stem. Glue the *two small orange* jack-o'-lanterns on the ends of the arms. Glue the *two black triangles* on the ends of the legs to make feet.

"Make your Pumpkin Man dance by moving his arms and legs."

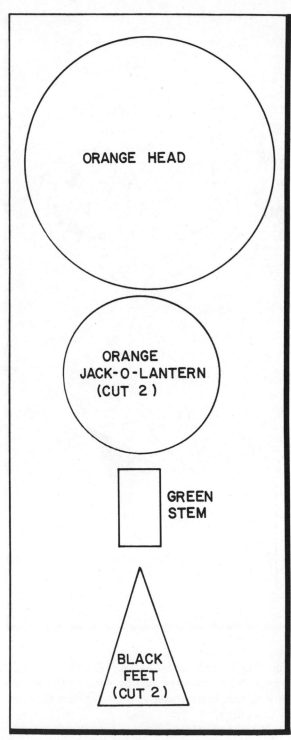

Fig. 10-4. Patterns for the Dancing Pumpkin Man.

ORANGE HEAD

ORANGE
JACK-O-LANTERN
(CUT 2)

GREEN
STEM

BLACK
FEET
(CUT 2)

## PAPER WITCH

A Paper Witch can also be made for Halloween (Fig. 10-6).

### Skills to Teach

Teach children 2 years old and up:

- The colors *black, green,* and *orange*
- The *triangle, rectangle, circle,* and *square* shapes
- How to draw a face
- Gluing skills

Teach children 4 years old and up:

- Cutting skills
- How to fringe and pleat

### Materials List

- Black, orange, and green construction paper
- A ruler and pencil
- Scissors
- Glue
- A black narrow-tipped marker

### Directions

For each Witch, cut two strips 1 × 9 inches from a sheet of black construction paper for the Witch's legs. Cut a triangle 9 × 11 × 11 inches from the remaining paper for the body. Use the black scraps that are left to trace two black triangles for hair, two black triangle shoes, two black rectangle arms 1 × 5 1/2 inches, and a narrow black hat brim 1/4 × 8 inches (Fig. 10-7).

Trace a green circle face, an orange broomstick 1/2 × 10 inches and an orange square 2 × 2 inches for the broom's bristles.

Cut these shapes out for children younger than 4 years. Children 4 years old and up can cut their own. Show them how to fringe the two triangles for the hair and the orange square for the broom bristles.

Instruct the children by saying: "Glue the *black triangle* hair and the *black triangle* hat to the *green circle* Witch's face. Add the narrow black hat brim.

"Use the marker to draw a mean witch face, or draw a nice face if you wish to make a nice witch.

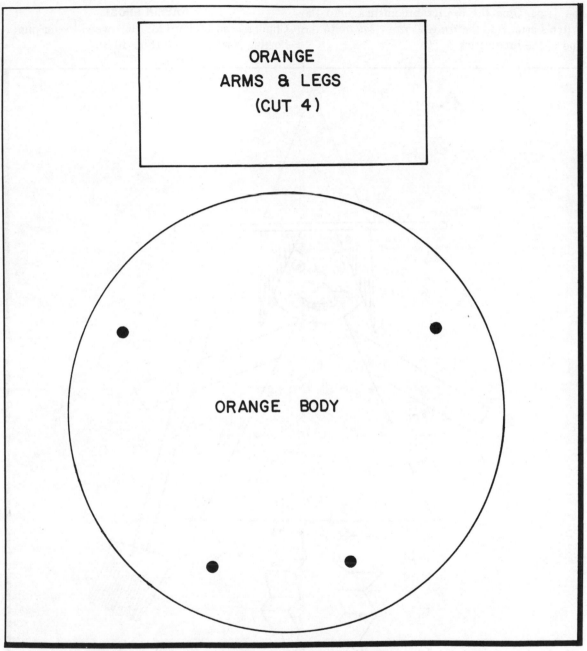

ORANGE
ARMS & LEGS
(CUT 4)

ORANGE BODY

Fig. 10-5. The patterns for the arms, legs, and body of the Dancing Pumpkin Man.

"Glue the Witch's head to the top of the *large black triangle*. Glue the two *short black rectangles* to the top of her body for arms.

"*Pleat* the two *long black rectangles* at 1-inch intervals. Glue them to the bottom of the triangle body to form legs." You will need to help them with the measurements.

"Glue two *black triangle* shoes to the ends of

the legs. Glue the *orange* broomstick onto the Witch's arm. Add the *fringed orange square* to the end of the broomstick."

## NAPKIN GHOST

Children can prepare for Halloween by making a floating Napkin Ghost (Fig. 10-8).

Fig. 10-6. The Paper Witch.

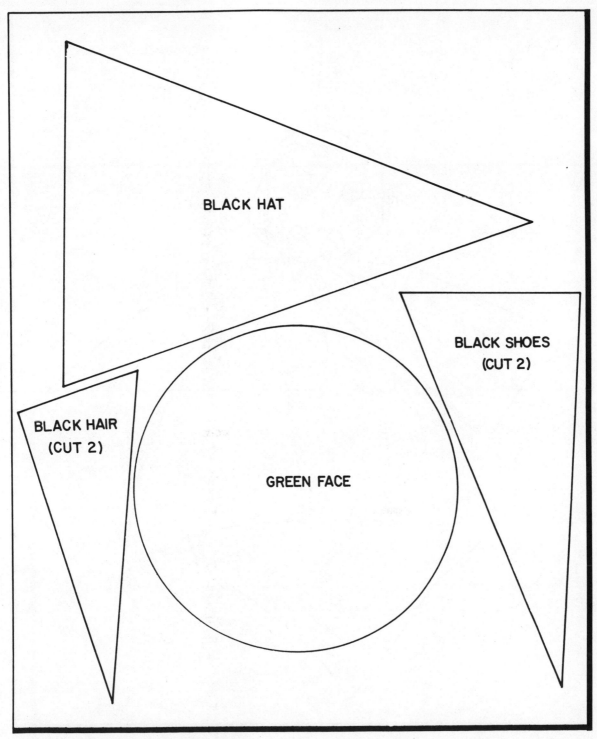

Fig. 10-7. The patterns to make the Paper Witch.

Fig. 10-8. The Napkin Ghost.

### Skills to Teach

Teach children 2 years old and up:

- The colors *black* and *white*
- The meaning of *unfold,* and *in the center*
- How to draw a face

Teach children 4 years old and up:

- To follow directions
- How to tie a knot

### Materials List

- A white napkin for each ghost (generic napkins work well)
- 2 cotton balls for each head
- White thread
- A black skinny marker

### Directions

Give each child a napkin, two cotton balls, and a white thread about 24 inches long.

Tell them to *unfold* the napkin and lay it flat on the table.

Tell them to put the two *white* cotton balls *in the center* of the *white* napkin. Show them how to pull the napkin up and pinch it shut around the cotton balls to make the ghost's head.

Help them tie the end of the *white* thread around the ghost's neck, just under the cotton balls.

Each child can draw a face on the ghost with the skinny *black* marker.

Hold the ghosts up by the string to make them float around, or tape them in a window or a doorway.

### EGG CARTON SPIDER

Another use for an empty egg carton is to make Egg Carton Spiders (Fig. 10-9).

### Skills to Teach

Teach children 2 years old and up:

- How to draw a face
- To count to *4*
- That spiders have 8 legs
- To count to *8*

Fig. 10-9. The Egg Carton Spider.

## Materials List

• 2-9 inch chenille pipe cleaners or 4 regular pipe cleaners from the supermarket for each spider
• Scissors
• A styrofoam egg carton
• A black permanent marker. (A laundry marker.)
• A needle
• Black thread
• Buttons

## Directions

Cut the chenille pipe cleaners in half with scissors to make four pipe cleaners or cut four regular pipe cleaners into 4 1/2-inch lengths for each spider.

Carefully cut out one egg cup from the styrofoam egg carton. Children 5 years old and up can cut their own.

Each child can draw a fierce-looking face on the egg cup with the laundry marker.

Give them each four pipe cleaners. Count them out loud with them to make sure that they have the right number.

Talk about spiders. Tell them that spiders have eight legs, while insects have only six legs. Since a spider has eight legs, it is not an insect (bug), but an arachnid (a-răk-nĭd). Spiders are in the same class as ticks, scorpions, and mites, all of which have eight legs. You may think this is too much information for a 2-year-old, but it isn't. If he is exposed to such ideas now, he will learn as much as he is ready to learn. This complex idea will not be strange to him when he is introduced to it again at a later age.

Tell your children to turn their egg cup over. Help them insert a pipe cleaner through one side, across the middle of the egg cup, and through the other side so that it extends evenly on both sides of the cup. One pipe cleaner makes two legs. Repeat this step for the remaining three pipe cleaners.

Bend the pipe cleaners downward to look like spider legs. Count the spider legs out loud with each child: "One... two... three... four... five... six... seven... eight." Then ask, "How many legs does your spider have? That's right. It has eight legs!"

Thread the needle with black thread. Thread the button onto the end of the thread and tie it into place.

Sew the needle through the inside top of each egg cup. Pull it until the button is snug against the inside top. Cut off the needle. The spider now has a black "web" from which to hang.

## HALLOWEEN HOUSE PICTURE

As the children make this Halloween picture, they'll recognize the pumpkin and ghosts from previous projects (Fig. 10-10).

## Skills to Teach

Teach children 2 years old and up:

• The colors *black, blue, purple, yellow, orange, green,* and *white*
• The names of the *triangle, rectangle, square,* and *circle* shapes
• Gluing skills
• The meaning of *next to, tall, short, large,* and *small*
• How many make *3*
• To count to *4*

Teach children 4 years old and up:

• Cutting skills
• Assembling skills: putting things together
• Alphabetical order

## Materials List

• Black, blue, purple, yellow, orange, and green construction paper
• A pencil and ruler
• Scissors
• Glue
• White facial tissue
• A black, narrow-tipped marker

## Directions

Each child will use a sheet of black construction paper for the background of this picture. With

Fig. 10-10. The Halloween House Picture.

the pencil and ruler, draw the following for each child:

    —2 blue rectangles 1 1/2" × 3 1/2"
    —1 blue rectangle 1 1/2" × 2"
    —1 blue square 3" × 3"
    —4 black rectangles 1/2" × 1"
    —4 black squares 1/2" × 1/2"
    —2 white facial tissue squares 3" × 3"
    —1 green rectangle 1/4" × 1/2"

Now use the pattern in Fig. 10-11 to trace a yellow circle moon, an orange circle jack-o'-lantern, three large purple triangle roofs, and one small purple triangle roof for each picture.

Cut these shapes out for the children, or let them cut their own if they are at least 4 years old.

Give these pieces to each child. To make the Halloween House Picture, instruct them by saying:

"*A*. Glue the *blue square* near the bottom of the *black* construction paper.

"*B*. Glue the two *tall blue rectangles* next to the *blue square,* one on each side.

"*C*. Glue the *short blue rectangle above* the *blue square*.

"*D*. Glue the *three large purple triangles* above the three *blue rectangles* to make roofs.

"*E*. How many *black rectangles* do you have? Count them with me. One... two... three... four. How many *black* rectangles? *Four*. Glue the *four black rectangles* on the house to make a door and windows.

"*F*. Glue the *small purple triangle* above the *black rectangle* door.

"*G*. How many *black squares* do you have? Let's count them." Count to four out loud with the child. "How many *black squares*? *Four*. Glue these four black squares on both sides of the door to make more windows.

"*H*. Use the black marker to draw a jack-o'-

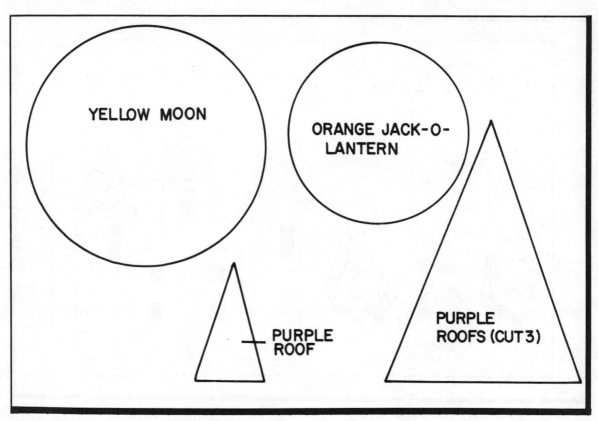

Fig. 10-11. The patterns for the Halloween House Picture.

lantern on the orange circle. Glue the jack-o-lantern *next to the house.*

"I. Add the *small green rectangle* for a pumpkin stem.

"J. Glue the *large yellow circle* in the sky for a moon.

"K. Pinch each *white* facial tissue square in the middle and squeeze it to make a ghost. Glue the two *white* ghosts near the jack-o'lantern.

"L. Use the black marker to draw tiny faces on the ghosts."

### PUMPKIN LADY

Another Halloween craft is the Pumpkin Lady (Fig. 10-12).

### Skills to Teach

Teach children 2 years old and up:

• The letter *I*, *V*, and *W*

• The colors *black, green,* and *orange*
• The *circle* and *triangle* shapes
• Gluing skills
• How many make *3*
• To count to *4* and *8*

Teach children 4 years old and up:

• Cutting skills
• Alphabetical order

### Materials List

• Black, green, and orange construction paper
• Yarn, any color
• Scissors
• Glue
• A pencil and ruler

### Directions

Use the patterns in Figs. 10-13 and 10-14 to

trace an orange circle head, a green triangle dress, three black triangles for eyes and nose, and a black mouth for each Pumpkin Lady.

Fold a piece of black construction paper in half. Trace the letter *V* and the letter *W* by placing the pattern on the fold and tracing around it (Fig. 10-13). Cut these letters out through both thicknesses of paper, then unfold the letters.

To make the letter *I*, use pencil and ruler to draw a black rectangle 1 × 9 inches. To make the hair, cut eight pieces of yarn, each 8 inches long.

Cut everything out for younger children. Chil-

Fig. 10-12. The Pumpkin Lady.

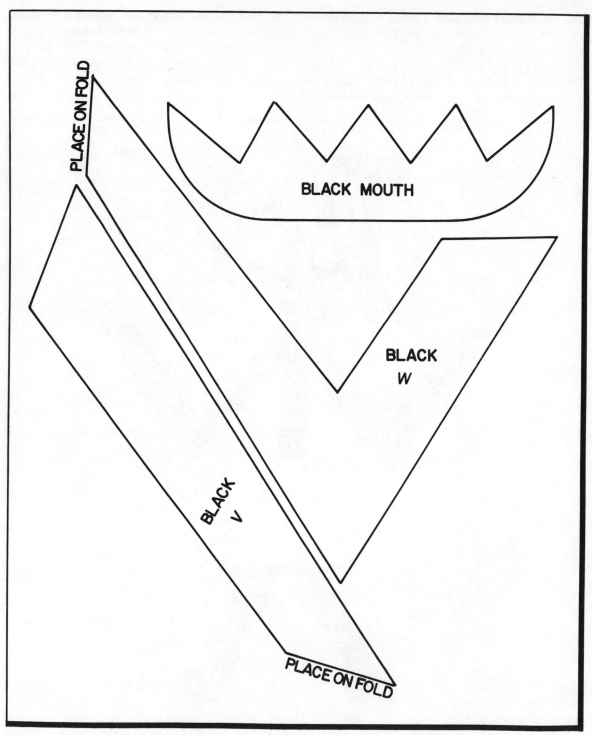

Fig. 10-13. Some patterns needed to make the Pumpkin Lady.

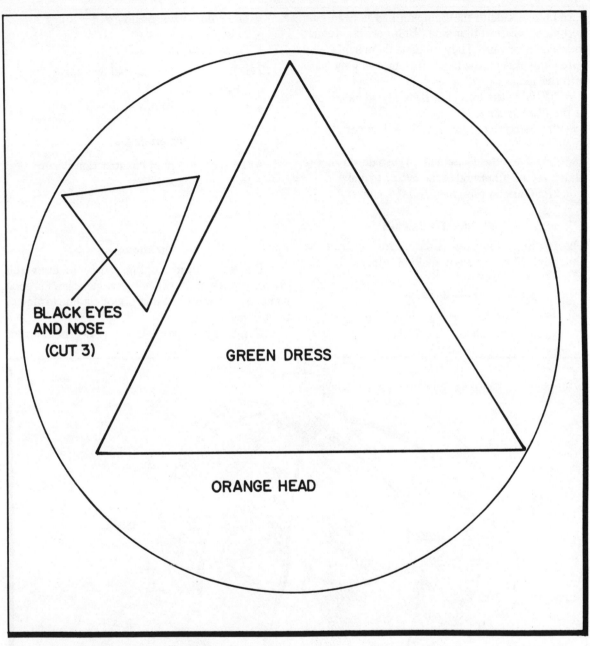

BLACK EYES
AND NOSE
(CUT 3)

GREEN DRESS

ORANGE HEAD

Fig. 10-14. More patterns for the Pumpkin Lady.

dren 4 years old and up can do much of the cutting themselves. Give these pieces to the child and tell him the following:

"*A*. Glue the *three black triangles* on the *orange circle* head to make two eyes and a nose. Add the *black* mouth. Draw pumpkin lines on the head if you want to.

"*B*. Let's count the pieces of yarn." Count to *eight* out loud with each child. "How many pieces do you have? *Eight* pieces of yarn. Glue *four* pieces of yarn on one side of the Pumpkin Lady's head, and *four* pieces on the other side."Help each child count four pieces of yarn. They can glue them in place by spreading glue on the head, then pressing the yarn into the glue.

"*C*. Glue the Pumpkin Lady's head on the end of the *black letter I*.

"*D*. Glue the *black letter W* below her chin to make arms.

"*E*. Turn the *black letter V* upside down and glue it on the other end of the *letter I* to make legs.

"*F*. Glue on the *green triangle* skirt.

### TEN-CIRCLE PUMPKIN

The 10-Circle Pumpkin is an interesting craft the children will really enjoy making (Fig. 10-15).

#### Skills to Teach

Teach children 2 years old and up:

- The *circle* and *rectangle* shapes
- The colors *orange* and *green*
- Gluing skills
- To count to *10*

Teach children 4 years old and up:

- Cutting skills
- The meaning of *in half*

#### Materials List

- Orange and green construction paper
- Ruler and pencil
- Scissors
- Glue

#### Directions

Use the pattern in Fig. 10-16 to draw ten orange circles and a green rectangle stem for each pumpkin. Draw a 2 1/2-inch slit or cut line in nine of the circles.

Cut these shapes out for younger children.

Fig. 10-15. The 10-Circle Pumpkin.

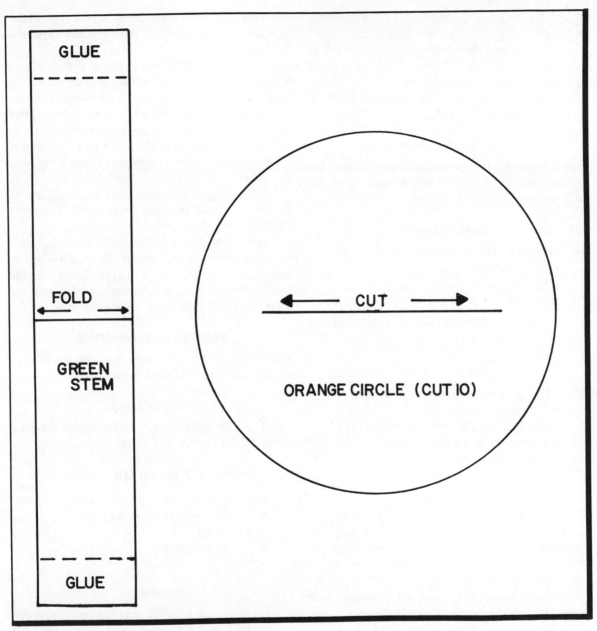

Fig. 10-16. The patterns for the 10-Circle Pumpkin.

Children 4 years old and up should be encouraged to cut their own.

Using the cut line as a guide, cut a slit in nine of the circles.

Instruct your children by saying, "Let's see how many *orange circles* you have. Count them with me." Count the ten circles out loud with each child. Then ask, "How many circles do you have? That's right, you have *ten*. *Ten* circles.

"Fold the *green rectangle in half* to make a pumpkin stem. Fold the glue line outward so the stem can be glued.

"Glue the *green rectangle* stem in the middle of the *orange circle* that does *not* have a slit.

"Hold each of the *orange circles* that are left so that the slit opens like a mouth. Slide each circle onto the circle that has the stem."

When the Ten-Circle Pumpkins are finished, they will stand by themselves.

## BUY A PUMPKIN

This activity is a family tradition at our house. We cut the pumpkin outside when we can. When we can't we use the kitchen table.

### Skills to Teach

Teach children 2 years old and up:

- How to draw a face
- How to clean out a pumpkin
- What is in a pumpkin

Teach children 4 years old and up how to make a jack-o'-lantern.

### Materials List

- Newspaper to cover the kitchen table
- A pumpkin for each child
- Black or purple water-based markers
- A sharp knife for you to use
- A big tablespoon

### Directions

Take the children pumpkin-shopping. Let each child pick out his or her own pumpkin. Pumpkins are usually sold by the pound, so help them pick out ones in accordance with your budget.

Wipe the mud off the pumpkins when you return home. Spread thick layers of newspapers on a table, and set the pumpkins on them.

The children should choose the best side of their pumpkin. Then they can draw a face on it, using a water-based marker. The face does not have to be the traditional triangle-eyed jack-o'-lantern. They can draw any face they wish as long as it has two eyes, a nose, and a mouth. Two- and 3-year olds can draw very scary faces made only of circles!

Now it's your turn. Cut a large circle on the top of the pumpkin. Make a large "V" in the back of the pumpkin as part of the lid to show you how to put the lid back on.

Next, cut out the eyes, nose, and mouth as drawn by the child. Use a wet cloth or sponge to wipe away remaining traces of water-based marker.

Give the pumpkins back to the children. They can use a big tablespoon and their hands to scoop out the pulp and seeds. Use your knife to cut and scrape stubborn pulp so they can spoon it out. Cut the pulp from the inside of the lid.

When the jack-o'-lanterns are finished, ask the children to give you the seeds so they can be roasted.

A small warming candle can be set inside each jack-o'-lantern and lit, giving off an eerie glow. Supervise very closely, however. Blow out the candle after a few minutes of enjoyment, and never leave the child alone with the candle lit.

## ROASTED PUMPKIN SEEDS

A delicious treat can be made from the seeds of all the pumpkins the children have carved.

### Skills to Teach

Teach children 2 years old and up that pumpkin seeds can be cooked and eaten.

### Materials List

- Seeds from 1 or more pumpkins
- 2 tablespoons cooking oil
- A jelly roll pan
- A wooden spoon
- Salt

### Directions

Preheat oven to 350°F. Put the pumpkin seeds in a jelly roll pan that has sides on it. You do not have to remove all the pulp; just take away as much as you can.

Pour on 2 tablespoons cooking oil. Stir with a wooden spoon to coat all the seeds. Add more oil if necessary.

Roast in a 350°F oven for 40 minutes until the seeds begin popping and turn a golden brown.

Remove the seeds from pan and drain on paper towels. Salt to taste. Serve hot or cold.

## SPIDER BREAD

Mix the dough 1 1/2 hours before you want to bake it. This recipe makes enough dough for six spiders, but it can be doubled (Fig. 10-17).

### Skills to Teach

Teach children 2 years old and up:

- To sit still, listen, and follow directions
- How to measure, stir, and bake
- To be creative with dough

### Materials List

- A large bowl and a wooden spoon
- 1/4 cup warm water
- 1 package active dry yeast
- 3/4 cup lukewarm water
- 1/3 cup dry powdered milk
- 1/4 cup sugar
- 1/4 cup soft shortening
- 1 teaspoon salt
- 1 egg
- 3 1/2 cups flour

### Directions

Help the children measure 1/4 cup warm water into the large bowl. Add one package active dry yeast and stir until dissolved.

Help the children measure and add the remaining ingredients. They can take turns stirring the dough until it is mixed and smooth, or you can use an electric mixer with a dough hook and mix on slow speed for 2 minutes.

Cover the bowl with plastic wrap and let it rise in a warm place (85° F) for 1 hour.

Stir dough. Let it rise again, covered, for 30 minutes. Now it's ready to use.

Put aprons on the children, tied up high to keep flour off their tummies. Divide the dough into six (or 12) equal pieces by cutting it with a knife. Give a piece to each child. Give the children a little pile of flour to keep their dough from sticking to the tabletop.

Tell the children to divide their dough into two equal pieces. One of these pieces is the body for the Spider. Put the body in the middle of a greased baking pan.

The children should divide their remaining lump of dough into eight pieces by pulling the dough apart, or by cutting it with a pizza cutter.

Fig. 10-17. Spider Bread.

Tell them to roll each ball into a snake 4 inches long. Pinch each snake onto the Spider body. Cut or pull the tips off two legs. Stick the tips onto the Spider to make eyes.

Brush the Spiders with milk. Let them rise for 20 minutes. Bake at 400° F for 12 to 15 minutes.

## WITCH'S FINGERS

The longer and more crooked Witch's Fingers are, the better. It helps to have a smooth plastic cloth on your kitchen table for easy clean up.

### Skills to Teach

Teach children 2 years old and up:

- How to work with dough
- How to measure, stir, and bake
- To count to *5*
- How to print his or her own name

### Materials List

- A large bowl
- A wooden spoon
- 1 1/2 cups warm water
- 1 package dry yeast
- 1 teaspoon salt
- 1 tablespoon sugar
- 5 cups flour
- 1 egg + 1 tablespoon water
- Coarse salt or table salt
- Paper plates and pencils

### Directions

Preheat the oven to 350° F. The children can grease two cookie sheets or jelly roll pans.

Help the children measure the warm water into the large bowl. Add the dry yeast. Let them stir it with a wooden spoon. Help them measure and stir in the salt, sugar, and flour. Count the cups of flour out loud with them as they add it to the bowl: "One . . . two . . . three . . . four . . . five. How many cups of flour did we add? *FIVE!*"

Shape the dough into a ball. Put a small pile of flour in front of each child, and let them smooth it around on the tabletop. Give each a portion of dough.

To make Witch's Fingers they should pull off a piece of dough the size of a walnut (or cut it off with a pizza cutter) and roll it between their hands until it is 15 inches long. They will need to hold it up in the air as they roll it to this length. Lay the Witch's Fingers on the greased baking sheets. Make sure they do not touch each other.

Put the egg and 1 tablespoon water in a jar with a tight-fitting lid. Shake hard. The children can brush this glaze on the Witch's Fingers, using a pastry brush. Sprinkle the Fingers with coarse salt or table salt.

Bake at 350° F for 25 minutes. Loosen the Witch's Fingers from the pan with a metal spatula and separate them if necessary.

Give each child a paper plate and a pencil. Help each one write his or her name on their plate. Make sure they hold their pencils correctly and use uppercase and lowercase letters. Put each child's Witch's Fingers on his or her own plate to eat or to share.

### Witch's Bones

Loosen the Witch's Fingers from the pan after they have baked. Separate them if necessary. Return them to the turned-off oven and leave them there until cool. They should be as hard and dry as the Witch's Bones in a few hours. Don't serve them to anyone who has weak teeth.

# 11: November Crafts

Turkey, pilgrim, and Indian crafts help the children learn Thanksgiving traditions. Throughout the chapter, emphasis is on teaching visual-motor skills that help coordinate the eye and finger muscles, following directions in sequence, and learning shapes, colors, and sizes.

### READ-YOUR-NAME GAME

Play this game when giving the children paper plates for their cooking crafts, or paper cups for their drinks. Hold a plate or cup in front of you so everyone can see it.

Say, "I'm going to write someone's name on this plate (cup). If it is your name, raise your hand." Print a child's name on the plate or cup while spelling it out loud. "B-A-R-B-A-R-A. Whose name is this? That's right, Barbara. This is your plate (cup)." Give Barbara the plate or cup and repeat with the next child.

Some children will raise their hand for *every* plate or cup just to make sure they don't miss theirs. Eventually, though, they will learn to read not only their name, but also the names of all the other children present.

### CRAFT-TRAINING SKILLS TO LEARN

Preschool skills to practice in November include:

- Learning to recognize the colors and shapes
- Printing his or her name
- Drawing a face
- Counting to 10
- Stringing beads, another eye-hand coordination exercise
- Learning to cut, color, draw, and glue

### CONSTRUCTION PAPER INDIAN

Start off the month of November by teaching your children to make the Construction Paper Indian (Fig. 11-1).

#### Skills to Teach

Teach children 2 years old and up:

- The colors *brown* and *red*

Fig. 11-1. The Construction Paper Indian.

- The letters *T* and *X*
- Drawing and coloring skills
- Gluing skills
- How to write his or her name

Teach children 4 years old and up cutting skills.

- Ruler and pencil
- Scissors
- Glue
- Crayons
- Cellophane tape

## Materials List

- Brown and red construction paper

## Directions

For each Indian, use the pencil and ruler to draw the letter *T* on a sheet of brown construction

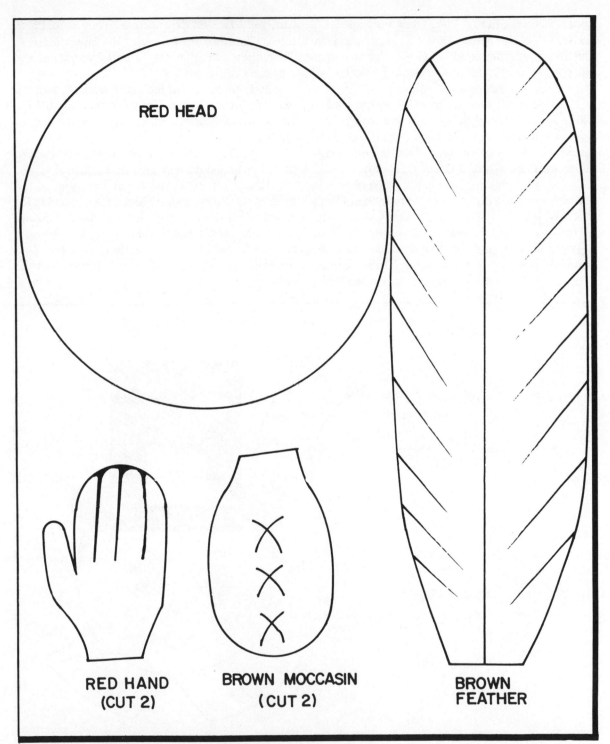

RED HEAD

RED HAND
(CUT 2)

BROWN MOCCASIN
(CUT 2)

BROWN
FEATHER

Fig. 11-2. The patterns to make the Construction Paper Indian.

paper, as shown in Fig. 11-1. Draw a triangle 5 1/2 inches tall at the bottom of the *T*, as shown. Give the T to your older child to cut out. You should do the cutting for the children under 4. *Do not* cut out the triangle at this time.

Use the pattern in Fig. 11-2 to trace a red circle head, two red hands, a brown feather, and two brown moccasins for each Indian. Cut these shapes out for your younger child, but encourage those over the age of 3 to cut their own.

Tell your children to snip the *brown letter T* all the way around with scissors to make the Indian's clothes look like buckskin. Then they should snip all the way around the *brown* feather slightly. Have cellophane tape ready if they snip too much and suddenly have two short feathers and half an Indian.

Tell them to use crayons to draw a headband, hair, and a face on the *red circle*. They should glue this Indian head to the top of the *brown letter T*. Then they can glue the two *red* hands on the crossbars of the *letter T*.

Help them cut out the *brown triangle*, forming two legs for the Indian. They can draw the *letter X* on the two moccasins, and glue them on the ends of the legs.

With crayons they can add a belt and beads to their Indian and draw fingers on the hands.

Help each child print his or her name on the front of the Indian's shirt. Make sure he holds his pencil or crayon correctly when writing or drawing, and that he uses uppercase and lowercase letters. If necessary, hold his hand lightly to help him do a good job. Spell his name out loud to him as he writes each letter.

Fig. 11-3. The Pilgrim Man.

## PILGRIM MAN

To help teach your children about Thanksgiving, help them make this Pilgrim Man (Fig. 11-3).

### Skills to Teach

Teach children 2 years old and up:

- The colors *white, black,* and *yellow*
- The *square* shape
- How to draw a face
- Gluing skills

Teach children 4 years old and up cutting skills.

### Materials List

- 9″ white paper plates. (Generic plates work well.)
- Scissors
- Crayons
- Glue

### Directions

Use the pattern to draw a triangle along the edge of each paper plate, as shown in Fig. 11-3. Cut the triangle out for younger children. Children 4 years old and up can cut their own after you have drawn it.

Cut the edge off the paper plate, leaving 2 pilgrim collars 3 1/2 inches wide, as shown in Fig. 11-3. This cut-off edging makes a cute pilgrim bonnet; just put it on a little girl's head like a headband.

Use the pattern in Fig. 11-4 to trace a black hat and a square yellow buckle for each Pilgrim. Once again, encourage children 4 years old and up to cut these shapes after you have drawn them.

Tell your children to glue the *square yellow* buckle on the *black* pilgrim hat.

Next they should draw hair and a face on the Pilgrim Man, and glue the hat on his head.

## PILGRIM WOMAN

You can help the boys make the Pilgrim Man just described, while the girls make this Pilgrim Woman (Fig. 11-5). If you wish, all the children can make one of each, and have a Pilgrim family.

### Skills to Teach

Teach children 2 years old and up:

- How to draw a face
- The color *white*

Teach children 4 years old and up cutting skills.

### Materials List

- 9″ white paper plates (Generic plates work well.)
- Scissors
- Crayons

### Directions

Use the pattern in Fig. 11-5 to draw a triangle and two rounded shapes along the edge of the paper plate for each Pilgrim Woman. Cut them out; children 4 years old and older can do their own cutting.

Your children can use crayons to draw a face and hair on the Pilgrim Woman. The top edge of the plate forms the woman's *white* hat. The two bottom edges form her *white* pilgrim collar.

---

### NOTE

Make masks from the Pilgrim Man and Pilgrim Woman by cutting out the eyes and tieing a string to both sides of the paper plate face. Tie the mask over the child's face.

---

## COFFEE CAN INDIAN DRUM

Indians played an important part in the first Thanksgiving. You can teach your children another aspect of their life with the Coffee Can Indian Drum (Fig. 11-6).

### Skills to Teach

Teach children 2 years old and up:

- The color *brown*
- To count to *10*
- Drawing skills
- Gluing skills

Teach children 4 years old and up how to cut paper *in half.*

Fig. 11-4. The patterns for the Pilgrim Man.

Fig. 11-5. The Pilgrim Woman.

Fig. 11-6. A Coffee Can Indian Drum.

## Materials List

- 2-pound coffee cans
- 2 plastic lids for each coffee can
- Brown construction paper
- Scissors
- Glue
- 10 dried beans for each can
- Cellophane tape
- Water-based markers

## Directions

Use a can opener to remove both ends from each coffee can. Give each child two sheets of brown construction paper (use paper grocery bags as a substitute), scissors, glue, beans, and markers.

Help them cut one sheet of *brown* paper *in half* by folding it across the middle, opening it, and cutting along the fold mark. You do the cutting for children under the age of 4 unless you have a lot of brown paper to waste.

171

To make the papers look like animal skin, the children should crumple them up, and then straighten them out again. They should glue the half-sheet on their cans first, by spreading glue on the paper, and pressing it smoothly onto the can.

Help each child spread glue on the whole sheet of *brown* paper, and press it smoothly onto the rest of the can. The whole *brown* sheet will overlap the half-sheet, completely covering the can. Fold and glue the excess paper firmly inside both ends of the can.

Cover one end with a plastic lid. Now they are ready to put the 10 beans in their Indian Drums. Ask them to count the beans out loud with you as they drop them in. Then ask, "How many beans did you put in your drum? *Ten* beans."

Close each drum with the remaining lid. Tape both lids shut all the way around with cellophane tape to prevent the children from removing the beans.

They can decorate the Indian Drum with markers. The designs on the drum in Fig. 11-6 are authentic North American Indian signs.

### CARDBOARD ROLL TOTEM POLE

Indians in the northwestern part of North America carved a wooden pole with emblems, or *totems*, that were important to their clan or family. The Cardboard Roll Totem Pole is made of authentic North American Indian designs (Fig. 11-7). Trace the designs, or let the children design their own "totems".

### Skills to Teach

Teach children 2 years old and up coloring and gluing skills.

Teach children 4 years old and up:

- Tracing and cutting skills
- Facts about Indian totems

### Materials List

- Paper towel cardboard rolls
- 3 different colors of construction paper
- Water-based markers and crayons
- Scissors
- Glue

Fig. 11-7. The Cardboard Roll Totem Pole.

### Directions

The children can trace the three totem patterns in Figs. 11-8 through 11-10 or design their own totems.

Help them cut out the totems and color them. You must cut out the three totems for children younger than 4.

172

Fig. 11-8. One of the patterns to make the Totem Pole.

Help them spread glue on a sheet of construction paper, and press it onto the cardboard roll, covering the roll completely.

Now they can glue the totems onto the roll, overlapping them a little. In Fig. 11-7, the top totem is glued to the back of the second totem to give it extra height and an interesting look.

## INDIAN BEADS

The children can dress up as Indians for Thanksgiving after they've made necklaces and bracelets of Indian Beads (Fig. 11-11). They'll have fun and learn at the same time.

### Skills to Teach

Teach children 2 years old and up:

- The colors *red, blue, yellow,* and *green*
- How to string beads

### Materials List

- Short straight pasta called *chili macs* or *ditali*
- Red, blue, yellow, and green liquid food dye

Fig. 11-9. Another pattern for the Totem Pole.

- 4 jars with lids
- Paper towels
- 2 or 3 pipe cleaners for each child
- A piece of yarn 30″ long for each child
- Feathers (marabou feathers from a craft store, or any others)
- Glue

**Directions**

Divide the pasta among the four jars, filling each jar about 1/3 full. Pour a few drops of liquid food dye in the jars, a different color for each one. Put the lid on tightly.

Give these jars to the children to shake vigorously. The food dye will spread among all the little

Fig. 11-10. The pattern for the bottom of the Totem Pole. Note that both parts of the pattern must be made as one.

Fig. 11-11. Indian Beads.

pasta pieces. If the lid comes off it will spread all over the children.

Open each jar and pour the colored pasta onto paper towels. Let them dry.

To string the Indian Beads, bend the end of a pipe cleaner and tie on the yarn. Squeeze it to the rest of the pipe cleaner to keep the yarn from falling off it.

Help the children tie one pasta on the other end of the yarn to keep the Indian Beads from falling off as they are strung. Put the beads where everyone can reach them.

As the children string the pasta beads onto their yarn, comment on the colors they are using. You might say, "Barbara, I see lots of *red* beads on your Indian necklace. You must like that color." Or, "Terry, why don't you add some *yellow* beads to

your necklace?" Or, "Mary, the *blue* Indian beads that you're stringing are the same color as the shirt you're wearing."

When the children have filled their yarns with beads, remove the pipe cleaner and tie the yarn ends together to form necklaces.

The children can add a feather or two by dipping the end of the feather in glue, and inserting it into several beads.

They can make bracelets by stringing more beads on a pipe cleaner, and twisting it into a circle. Small children need only one pipe cleaner to fit around their wrist; larger children can twist two pipe cleaners together to make a larger bracelet.

### CIRCLE TURKEY

Teach the children about the part the turkey plays in

Thanksgiving, while you teach them colors and shapes. You can use the Circle Turkeys as decorations for your feast, as well (Fig. 11-12).

### Skills to Teach

Teach children 2 years old and up:

• The colors *red, yellow, brown, orange,* and *black*

     • The *circle* and *diamond* shapes

• Gluing skills

Teach children 4 years old and up:

• Cutting skills
• To follow directions

### Materials List

• Red, yellow, brown, orange, and black construction paper
• Scissors

Fig. 11-12. The Circle Turkey.

- Glue
- Several feathers (Use marabou craft feathers or any others.)

### Directions

Use the pattern in Fig. 11-13 to draw five circles of graduated diameter in the colors suggested, or gather a variety of kitchen objects to trace around, each a little larger than the last. You could use a vitamin bottle lid, a drinking glass, a coffee cup, a sour cream container, a cereal bowl, and a large pot lid.

After you have drawn the circles, let the children cut them out. You must do the cutting for

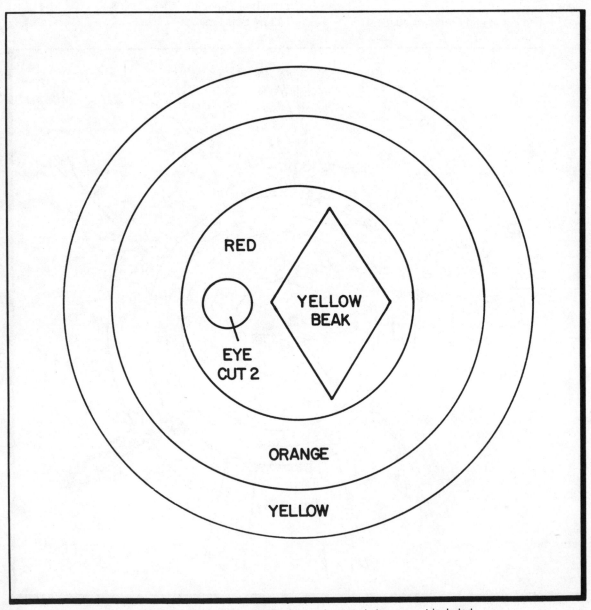

RED

YELLOW
BEAK

EYE
CUT 2

ORANGE

YELLOW

Fig. 11-13. The patterns to make the Circle Turkey. Note the two largest circles are not included.

Fig. 11-14. More patterns for the Circle Turkey.

children under 4 years of age.

Use the patterns in Figs. 11-13 and 11-14 to draw two black eyes, a yellow beak, two yellow feet, a red wattle, and a red neck for each turkey. Cut these shapes out or let the children do it. Then tell the children the following:

"*First*, glue the *brown circle* in the middle of the *largest orange circle*.

"*Second*, glue the *yellow circle* in the middle of the *brown circle*.

"*Third*, glue the *small orange circle* on the *yellow circle*.

"*Fourth*, fold the *red* neck so that it looks like the *letter Z*. Put the glue on the two ends of the neck. Glue the neck in the middle of the *small orange circle*. then glue the *red circle* head on the neck.

"*Fifth*, glue the two *little black circle* eyes on the *red circle* head. Fold the *yellow diamond* beak in half. Glue it below the *black circle* eyes.

"*Sixth*, glue the two *yellow* feet between the *brown circle* and the *large orange circle*.

"*Seventh*, dip some feathers in glue and *insert* them between the *brown circle* and the *large orange circle*."

## TURKEY WITH PAPER FEATHERS

Another turkey project the children can make is this Turkey with Paper Feathers (Fig. 11-15).

### Skills to Teach

Teach children 2 years old and up:

- The colors *yellow, brown, red,* and *orange*
- The *triangle* shape
- Gluing skills
- To count to *9*

Teach children 4 years old and up cutting skills.

Fig. 11-15. The Turkey with Paper Feathers.

## Materials List

• Yellow, brown, red, and orange construction paper
• Construction paper in any other colors
• Scissors
• Glue

## Directions

For each turkey, use the pattern in Fig. 11-16 to trace a brown head, a red wattle, two orange feet, an orange triangle beak, and nine feathers in any colors. Draw around a pot lid or bowl to make a 7 3/4-inch diameter body with triangle wings drawn near the bottom; make this body yellow.

Cut out these shapes for younger children. Children 4 years old and up should be encouraged to cut their own.

Ask the children to count the turkey feathers out loud with you to see how many they have. After counting to nine with them, ask, "How many feathers do you have? You have *nine*."

Help the children glue the *nine* feathers on the

back of the *yellow* turkey body. They should glue on the two *orange* feet and the *brown* turkey head, as shown in Fig. 11-15. Help them add the *orange triangle* beak.

They can glue the *red* wattle on. Then each child can draw eyes on his or her turkey.

## PINE CONE TURKEY

Buy multicolored marabou feathers at the craft

Fig. 11-16. The patterns for the Turkey with Paper Feathers. Note the instructions for making the body.

Fig. 11-17. The Pine Cone Turkey.

store, or use any feathers you can find for this Pine Cone Turkey (Fig. 11-17). You can use them as centerpieces at your Thanksgiving Feast.

### Skills to Teach

Teach children 2 years old and up:

- The color *red*
- Gluing skills

Teach children 4 years old and up:

- Cutting skills
- The meaning of *wattle*

### Materials List

You can buy the first three items in a craft store:

- Feathers

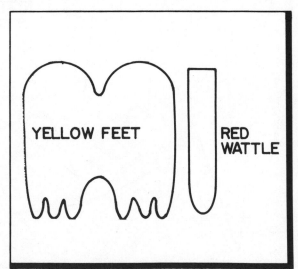

Fig. 11-18. The patterns to make the Pine Cone Turkey.

- Red felt
- 2 paste-on movable eyes, size 4MM, for each turkey
- A pine cone 2″ or bigger for each turkey
- Construction paper
- White glue
- Scissors

### Directions

Use the pattern provided in Fig. 11-18 to trace turkey feet onto construction paper. Trace a wattle for each turkey onto red felt. Cut these shapes out. Encourage children 4 years old and up to cut their own.

Give each child a pine cone, paper feet, a wattle, two eyes, and glue. Place the feathers where all the children can reach them.

Tell the children to turn the pine cone on its side, dip the end of each feather in glue, and stick it into the pine cone near the stem end. They can add as many feathers as they wish, depending on the size of the feathers.

Fig. 11-19. The Paper Plate Turkey.

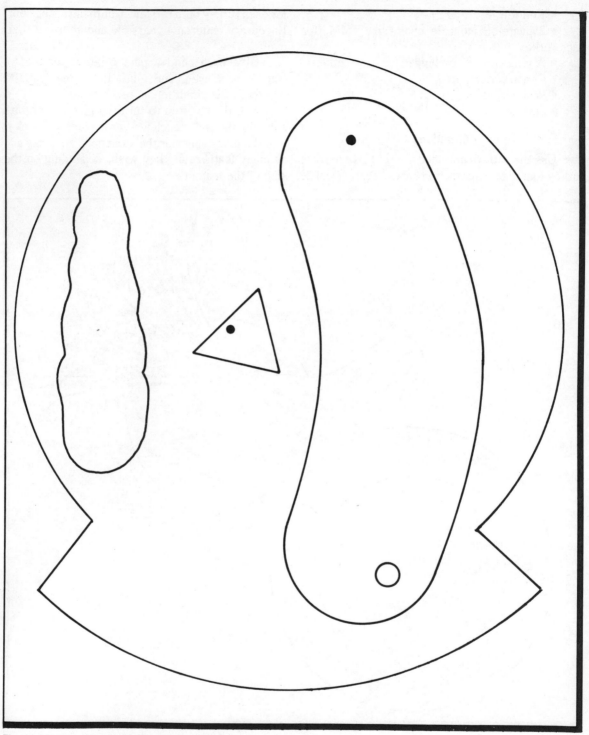

Fig. 11-20. The patterns for the Paper Plate Turkey.

On a real turkey the *wattle* is the fleshy red piece that hangs down over the turkey's beak. Help the children glue the *red* felt wattle to the side of the pine cone tip so that the tip looks like the turkey's beak.

Next they should glue the eyes, one on each side of the turkey's beak. Put lots of glue on the paper feet and stick them to the bottom of each turkey so they will stand up. Let them dry all day or overnight.

If, despite their feet, the turkeys tip over because of their heavy tail, glue their feet to a piece of cardboard and pretend it's a barnyard. The children can draw corn and a water trough for their turkeys on the cardboard. You could also lean the turkey against something.

### PAPER PLATE TURKEY

Another turkey project that can stand is this Paper Plate Turkey (Fig. 11-19).

### Skills to Teach

Teach children 2 years old and up:

- The colors *red* and *yellow*
- The *triangle* shape
- Coloring skills
- To count to *5*

Teach children 4 years old and up cutting skills.

### Materials List

- 2-9″ white paper plates for each turkey. (Buy generic; they make good crafts.)
- Red and yellow construction paper
- Metal paper fasteners
- 5 marabou craft feathers or other feathers for each turkey
- Scissors
- Glue
- Crayons and a pen

### Directions

For each turkey, use the pattern in Fig. 11-20 to draw the turkey head and body on the paper plate. On construction paper, trace a red wattle and a yellow triangle beak. Cut them out for the younger child; encourage children 4 years old and up to cut their own.

Use a pen to draw the turkey's feathers, feet, and eyes, as shown in Fig. 11-19. Your children can color the turkey head and body with crayons.

Tell them to glue the *yellow triangle* on the turkey's head to make a beak. Then they can glue the *red* wattle over the beak so that the wattle hangs down.

Help them fasten the turkey's head to its body with the paper fastener. They can glue on the *five* feathers by dipping them in the glue one at a time, and sticking them on the front of the turkey's body.

Ask them, "How many feathers did you glue on the turkey? Let's count them and find out." Count the feathers out loud with them. Then ask, "How many feathers? *Five* feathers on your turkey."

To make the Paper Plate Turkey stand up, cut a rectangle 3 × 4 inches from the middle of the second paper plate. In the center of this rectangle cut a vertical slit 2 1/2 inches long. Fold the rectangle horizontally. Insert the bottom of the turkey into the slit.

# 12: December Crafts

Christmas crafts wrap up the year and this book. Many of the crafts, such as the tree ornaments, are suitable for gifts, but my favorite is the Holly Leaf Napkin Ring. A set of them makes a beautiful gift for a special friend or teacher. If you cut the felt, even the youngest child can help glue them together.

## A SWEET ORNAMENT

The Sweet Gum Ornament has nothing to do with chewing gum. The Sweet Gum is a shade tree found in the eastern United States. It has star-shaped leaves with five to seven points on them, and it turns a lovely scarlet and gold color in the fall.

If you're lucky enough to live near one, or if you know someone who does, collect *gum balls,* the dark brown spiny seed pods which fall off the tree in autumn. Store them in a paper bag until they dry. Don't put them in plastic, or they will mold.

A few years ago my children and I traveled with my husband to a business conference in New Jersey. There were Sweet Gum trees all around the tennis courts at the conference center. The children gathered the fattest gum balls and we brought them home to Illinois in a hotel laundry bag. The locals thought we were crazy, but at Christmas time we had enough gum balls for a whole Brownie troop to make ornaments.

## CRAFT-TRAINING SKILLS TO LEARN

The Sweet Gum Ornament not only looks nice, it also provides a good lesson in visual discrimination as the children try to find every little hole in the seed pod. It also provides practice in eye-hand coordination as they stick a glue-coated toothpick in the tiny hole.

Other Craft-training skills to practice while preparing for Christmas include:

- Following directions
- Learning the meaning of *first* through *seventh*
- Learning the meaning of *above, below, inside,* and *close together*
- How to fringe and to tie a knot
- How to use tape and glitter
- Recognizing the colors and shapes

- Putting things together
- How to cut and glue
- How to write "Merry Christmas"

## PAPER PLATE WREATH

Wreaths are very much a part of the holiday season. Have the children make this craft early in December, and they can decorate the house all month long (Fig. 12-1).

### Skills to Teach

Teach children 2 years old and up:

- The colors *red* and *green*
- The *circle* shape

- Gluing skills
- To follow directions

Teach children 4 years old and up cutting skills.

### Materials List

- 1 sheet of green tissue gift wrap paper for each wreath
- White 9″ paper plates. (Generic plates work very well.)
- White glue
- Typing paper and a pencil
- 1/2 sheet of red construction paper for each wreath
- Scissors

Fig. 12-1. The Paper Plate Wreath.

PLACE ON FOLD

Fig. 12-2. The pattern for the Paper Plate Wreath ribbon.

### Directions

Cut the center out of each paper plate, as shown in Fig. 12-1.

Cut the sheets of tissue gift wrap paper into 2-inch squares.

Pour a small amount of glue into saucers or old jar lids. Say to the children, "Press a *green* square firmly around your pointer finger, forming a tissue cup.

"Dip the bottom of the tissue cup into the glue. Press it onto the *circle* plate so that the *green* tissue sticks up. Do this with the rest of the *green* tissue squares, pressing them close together, until the *circle* plate is completely covered."

All the squares (approximately 120 of them) can be squeezed onto the paper plate for a full and fluffy wreath. Many children will not want to work

on this craft long enough to glue that many squares, however. Let them glue as many as they want, until the plate is partially covered all the way around. The wreath will still look pretty good.

To make the ribbon, use the typing paper and pencil to trace the ribbon pattern in Fig. 12-2. Cut it out. Fold the red construction paper in half. Place the ribbon pattern on the fold and trace around it. Cut it out for younger children, but encourage children 4 years old and up to cut their own ribbon.

Tell your children to glue the *red* ribbon near the bottom of the wreath. The finished wreaths can be hung on a doorknob or taped on a door.

### GROCERY SACK RUDOLPH

A delightful Christmas decoration is this Grocery Sack Rudolph, which can be made with simple materials (Fig. 12-3).

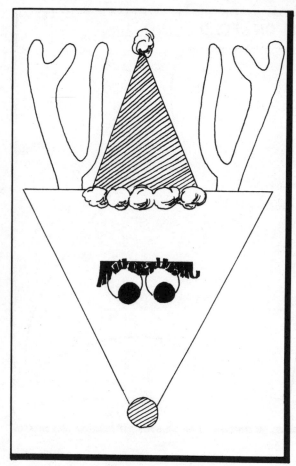

Fig. 12-3. The Grocery Sack Rudolph.

### Skills to Teach

Teach children 2 years old and up:

- The *rectangle, circle,* and *triangle* shapes
- The colors *red, white, brown,* and *black*
- Gluing skills
- The meaning of *close together* and *on top of*

Teach children 4 years old and up:

- Cutting skills
- How to fringe

### Materials List

- A large brown grocery sack for each Rudolph
- A pencil and ruler
- White typing paper

- Black and red construction paper
- Glue
- Scissors
- Cotton balls (optional)

### Directions

Using a pencil and ruler, measure and draw a triangle 12 × 14 × 14 inches on the plain side of each grocery sack, and cut them out.

For each child, use the pattern provided in Fig. 12-4 to draw and cut two antlers from the remainder of the grocery sack.

Trace and cut out two black rectangle eyelashes, two black circle eyeballs, two white eyes, and a red nose for each child. Encourage children 4 years old and up to do their own cutting.

Give the cutout pieces to the children and tell them the following:

"*First,* glue the *red circle* nose onto the point of the *brown triangle.*

"*Second,* glue the *white circle* eyes *close together* near the middle of the *triangle.* Glue the *black circle* eyeballs *on top of* the *white* eyes.

"*Third, fringe* the *black rectangle* eyelashes. Make them curl up by carefully wrapping the fringes around a pencil.

"*Fourth,* glue the *black* eyelashes on the eyes so that the eyes are partly covered.

"*Fifth,* glue the two *brown* antlers *on top of* Rudolph's head."

If you wish, add a skinny red triangle hat 11 inches tall and 5 1/2 inches wide at its base. Glue cotton balls along the brim of the hat. Glue tufts of cotton on both sides of the hat's pointed top. The weight of the cotton will make the top of the hat fall forward into Rudolph's face.

### PAPER PLATE SANTA

Have the children make this Paper Plate Santa to go with the Grocery Sack Rudolph (Fig. 12-5).

### Skills to Teach

Teach children 2 years old and up:

- The *circle* shape
- The colors *red, white, black,* and *blue*

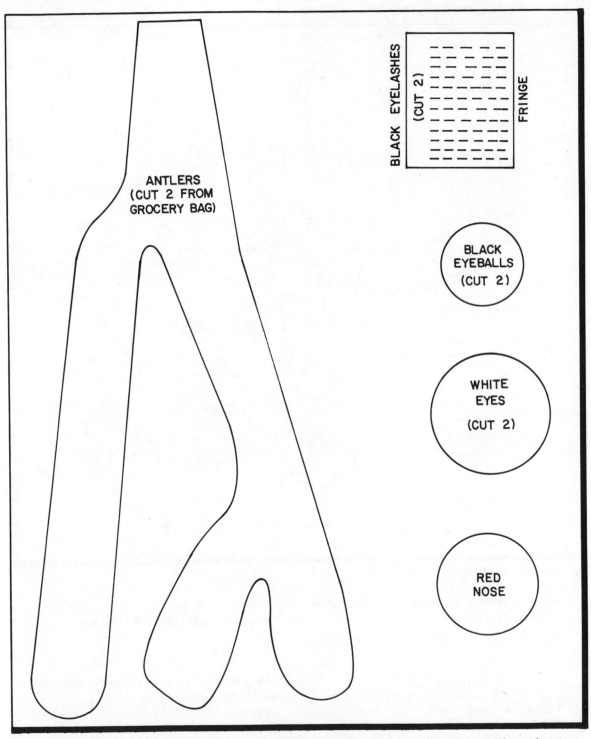

Fig. 12-4. The patterns to make the Grocery Sack Rudolph. Note that both parts of the antler pattern must be made as one.

Fig. 12-5. The Paper Plate Santa.

- The meaning of *on top of, below,* and *above*
- Gluing skills

Teach children 4 years old and up cutting skills.

## Materials List

- 9″ white paper plates
- Scissors
- White glue

- Red, black, and blue construction paper
- Cotton balls (also called cosmetic puffs)

## Directions

For each Santa, cut off part of the plate rim, as shown in Fig. 12-5.

Trace and cut out two blue circle eyes and two black circle eyeballs for each child. Cut out a red circle nose and a red mouth (Fig. 12-6). Children 4

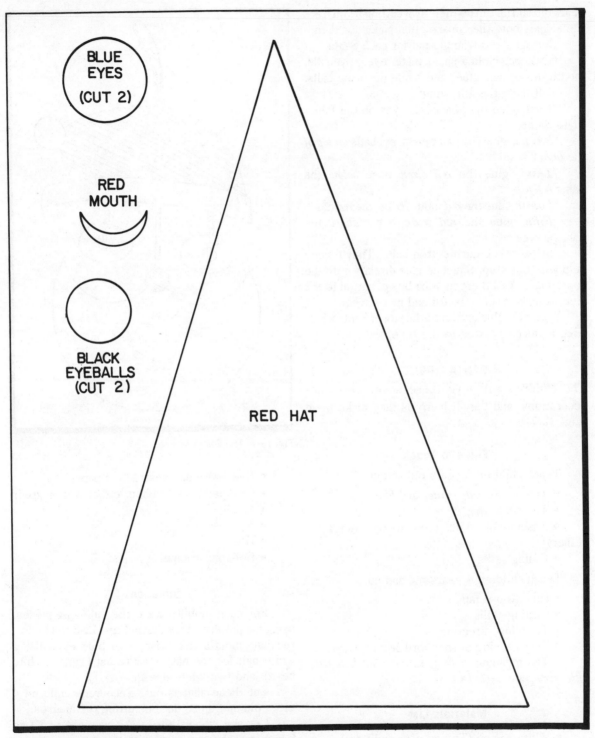

BLUE
EYES
(CUT 2)

RED
MOUTH

BLACK
EYEBALLS
(CUT 2)

RED HAT

Fig. 12-6. The patterns to make the Paper Plate Santa.

years old and up can do their own cutting if you trace the shapes onto the construction paper for them.

Cut out a red triangle hat for each Santa.

Give each child a paper plate, eyes, eyeballs, mouth, nose, hat, glue, and a pile of cotton balls.

Tell them the following:

"*First,* glue the *blue circle* eyes on the Paper Plate Santa.

"*Second,* glue the *black circle* eyeballs *on top of* the *blue* eyes.

"*Third,* glue the *red circle* nose *below* the Santa's eyes.

"*Fourth,* glue the *red* mouth *below* the *red* nose.

"*Fifth,* glue the *red triangle* hat *above* the Santa's eyes.

"*Sixth,* unroll each cotton ball." They'll need help with this step. Squeeze glue directly onto the paper plate. Tell them to stick bits of cotton to the glue to make Santa's beard and moustache.

"*Seventh,* glue cotton to the rim of Santa's hat. Glue a piece of cotton to the tip of the hat."

### SANTA MOBILE

The children will love these novel Christmas decorations, and they'll learn as they make them (Fig. 12-7).

### Skills to Teach

Teach children 2 years old and up:
- The colors *red, white,* and *blue*
- The *circle* shape
- Assembling skills (how to put things together)
- Gluing skills

Teach children 4 years old and up:
- How to use tape
- Cutting skills
- To follow directions
- The meaning of the word *behind*
- The meaning of *first, second, third, fourth, fifth, sixth,* and *seventh.*

### Materials List

- White paper. (Typing paper will do.)

Fig. 12-7. The Santa Mobile.

- Red and blue construction paper
- Crimped paper ribbon, either red or green
- Pencil
- Scissors
- Glue
- Cellophane tape

### Directions

For each mobile, trace the following pieces, using the patterns provided in Figs. 12-8 and 12-9: a red hat, mouth, and nose; two blue eyeballs; a white ball for the hat; a white hat brim; a white beard, and two white eyes.

Cut these shapes out. Encourage children 4 years old and up to do the cutting themselves.

Cut the ribbon into a 7-inch piece and two 3-inch pieces for each mobile.

Tell the children the following:

"*First,* glue the *white circle* ball on the tip of the *red* hat.

"*Second,* glue the *white* brim on the *red* hat.

"*Third,* glue the *blue circle* eyeballs on the *white* eyes.

"*Fourth,* glue the *red* nose and mouth on the *white* beard.

"*Fifth,* tape the 7-inch ribbon *behind* the beard and the hat brim, connecting them as shown in Fig. 12-7.

"*Sixth,* tape the 3-inch ribbons *behind* each eye. Then tape these ribbons *behind* the hat brim.

"*Seventh,* make a long loop from extra ribbon and tape it on the back of the cap." The Santa Mobile can be hung in a window or doorway.

## WALNUT TREE ORNAMENT

Children enjoy making Christmas Ornaments, so this craft is sure to be a hit (Fig. 12-10).

### Skills to Teach

Teach children 2 years old and up:

- Assembling skills
- How to use glitter
- The meaning of *inside*
- To follow directions

### Materials List

- A bag of walnuts in the shell
- A nutcracker and a nutpick
- 12" ribbon
- White glue
- Old newspapers
- Gold or silver spray paint
- Glitter, any color

### Directions

Use the nutcracker and nutpick to open the walnut along its seam so that it can be put back together again. Remove the nut meat. Children 5 years old and up can pry open their own walnuts. Younger children can pick out the nut meat if the nut is first cracked for them. You may need to open quite a few walnuts to make one or two ornaments because the shells shatter easily.

Help the children glue the shell halves back together with the two ends of the ribbon *inside* the shell and the rest of the ribbon sticking out the top to form a loop.

Lay the walnuts on old newspapers, either outside or in the garage. Spray them all over with gold or silver paint.

The children should pour glitter on them immediately so that the glitter will stick to the wet paint. Return the excess glitter to its container.

Let the ornaments dry overnight, then hang them by the ribbon.

## SWEET GUM ORNAMENT

The finished Sweet Gum Ornament looks like the sphere the baby was placed in for his trip to earth in the movie, *Superman* (Fig. 12-11). It makes a unique tree ornament that will stick by itself in the tree branches. No hook or ribbon is needed.

### Skills to Teach

Teach children 2 years old and up:

- To follow directions
- Eye-hand coordination
- Visual discrimination. (The child must find every hole in the gum ball.)
- The meaning of *insert*

### Materials List

- Gum balls from a Sweet Gum tree
- A box of round wooden toothpicks
- White glue
- Old newspapers
- Gold spray paint
- Glitter, any color

### Directions

Give the children the gum balls and some toothpicks. Pour a small amount of white glue into a saucer or old jar lid for each child.

Tell the children to dip the end of a toothpick

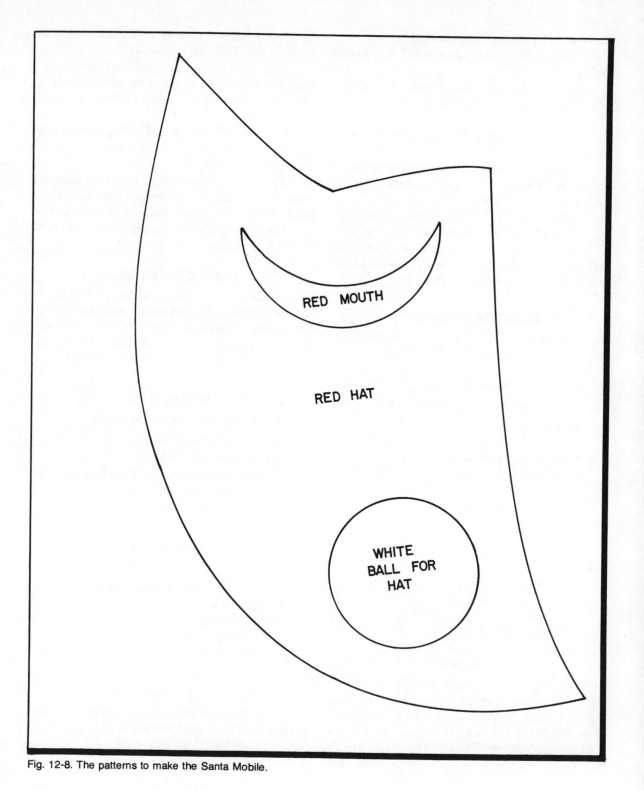

Fig. 12-8. The patterns to make the Santa Mobile.

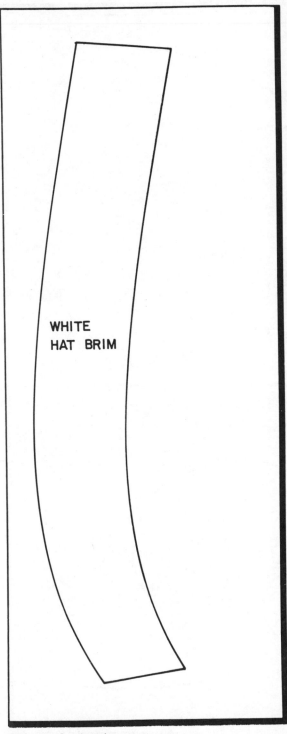

WHITE
HAT BRIM

Fig. 12-8. Continued.

into the glue and *insert* it into a hole in the gum ball. They should repeat this step until every hole is filled with one toothpick.

Now it's your turn. Spread old newspapers outside or on the floor of the garage. Spray the ornaments all over with gold paint.

While the paint is wet, let the children pour glitter on the ornaments. Shake off the excess and return it to its container. Let the ornaments dry overnight.

## SIX HOLLY LEAF NAPKIN RINGS

This craft requires a trip to the fabric or craft shop to buy red and green felt. It's included in this book because a set of six napkin rings is a lovely gift for a child to make and give for Christmas (Fig. 12-12).

### Skills to Teach

Teach children 2 years old and up:

- How many make *3*
- The *circle* shape
- Gluing skills
- Assembling skills
- How to use glitter

Teach children 8 years old and up cutting skills.

### Materials List

- Plain paper and a pencil
- 2 pieces of green felt 8 3/4" × 11 3/4" for 6 napkin rings
- 1 piece of red felt 8 3/4" × 11 3/4" or smaller for 6 napkin rings
- Contact cement or good quality white glue
- Glitter, any color
- Waxed paper
- Scissors sharp enough to cut felt

### Directions

For each napkin ring, use the plain paper and pencil to trace the pattern provided (Fig. 12-13). Cut out the pattern you have made. Fold one piece of green felt lengthwise. Place the Holly Leaf pattern on the felt, with the flat end of the pattern on the

197

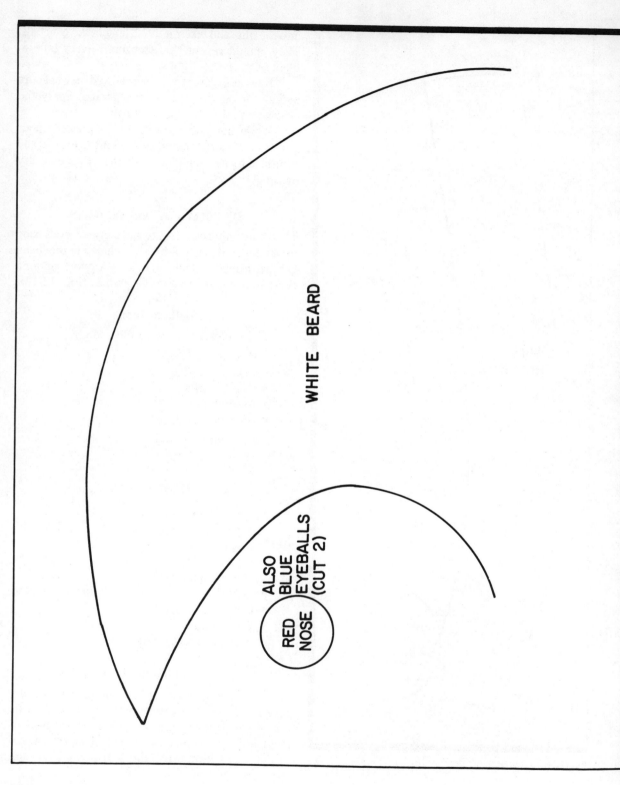

WHITE BEARD

ALSO
BLUE
EYEBALLS
(CUT 2)

RED
NOSE

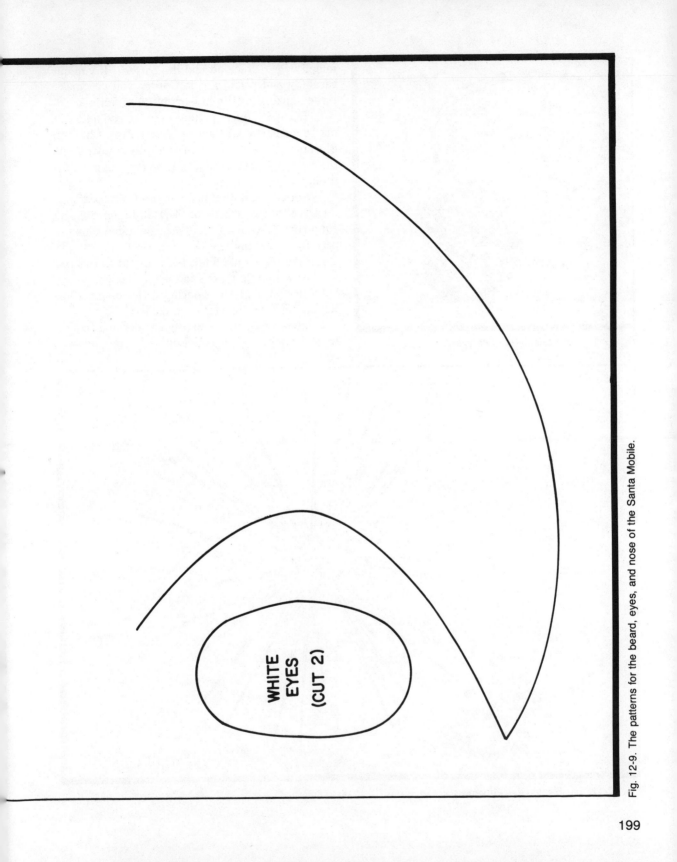

WHITE
EYES
(CUT 2)

Fig. 12-9. The patterns for the beard, eyes, and nose of the Santa Mobile.

Fig. 12-10. The Walnut Tree Ornament.

folded edge. Trace around the pattern. If you cut carefully and refold the felt once, you can make three napkin rings from each piece of felt.

Trace the Berry pattern onto the red felt. Cut out 18 red berries, 3 for each Napkin Ring. Children 8 years old and up can cut the felt themselves. Do the cutting yourself ahead of time for younger children.

Notice the dotted lines on the Holly Leaf pattern. These two pieces of the Holly Leaf must be cut off one leaf only. Cut a 1-inch slit (shown on the pattern) in the big leaf.

Give each child 6 felt holly leaves and 18 red felt berries. Help them slip the smaller end of the holly leaf through the 1-inch slit, forming a ring. Repeat until all the rings are made.

Lay a sheet of waxed paper under one Napkin Ring. Help each child count out three red felt ber-

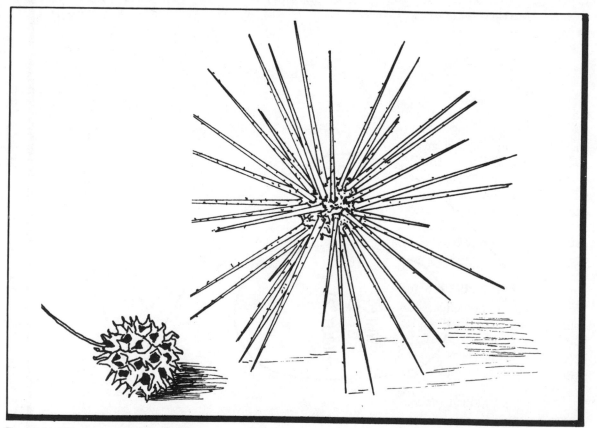

Fig. 12-11. The Sweet Gum Ornament.

Fig. 12-12. A Holly Leaf Napkin Ring.

ries. They should glue them onto the larger holly leaf, just above the slit, as shown in Fig. 12-12. Ask them what shape the red berries are *(circle)*. To teach them the circle shape, tell them to glue the *circles* onto the green holly leaf. Overlap the berries slightly, forming a triangular arrangement.

Spread glue directly from the tube or bottle along the edges of the holly leaves. Let them pour glitter onto the glue; the waxed paper will catch the excess, which can be returned to the glitter container. Gently shake off the extra glitter. Repeat until all six Napkin Rings are done. Let them dry overnight.

### PAPER PUNCH STOCKING

The children will be delighted to make their own Paper Punch Stocking (Fig. 12-14). When it is finished, they can hang them up and wait for them to be filled with Christmas goodies, or you can fill them right away.

### Skills to Teach

Teach children 2 years old and up:

- The colors *red* and *green*
- Lacing skills (good practice for eye-hand coordination)
- Drawing skills
- How to write his or her name

Teach children 6 years old and up cutting skills.

### Materials List

- Red and green construction paper
- Scissors
- A paper punch
- A 72″ piece of red or white or green yarn for each stocking
- A pipe cleaner for each stocking
- Crayons or water-based markers

### Directions

For each child, draw a stocking shape on one sheet of construction paper, as shown in Fig. 12-14. The stocking should be 6 1/2 inches wide at the top and 12 inches long. Draw a rounded heel and toe.

Cut the stocking shape out of both red and green paper by holding the two sheets together and

201

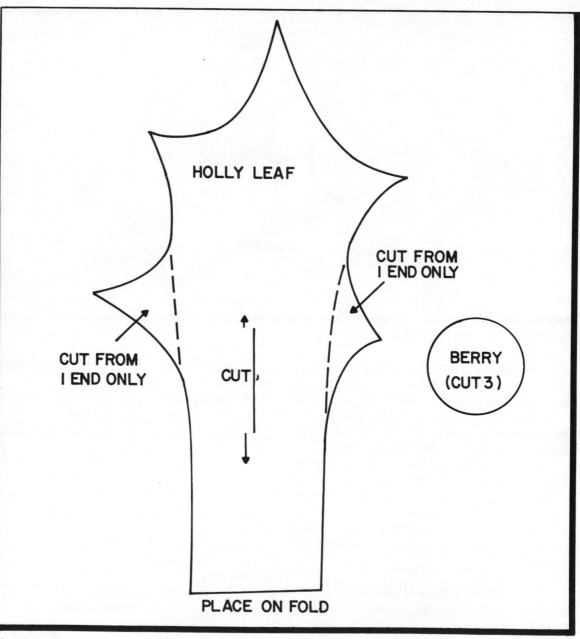

HOLLY LEAF

CUT FROM
I END ONLY

CUT FROM
I END ONLY

CUT

BERRY
(CUT 3)

PLACE ON FOLD

Fig. 12-13. The pattern for the Holly Leaf Napkin Rings.

cutting them as one. Encourage children 6 years old and up to cut their own.

Continue holding the two pieces together. Use the paper punch to make holes 1 inch apart around the edges of the stocking. Do not punch holes along the top of the stocking.

Tie a 72-inch piece of yarn to the end of a pipe cleaner. Twist the pipe cleaner back on itself to hold the yarn.

Give two paper stockings and the yarn to each

child. Tell them to lace the *red* and *green* stocking shapes together, starting at the top and lacing all the way around.

Then they can decorate the stockings with crayon or marker drawings. They should print their names neatly at the top, using uppercase and lowercase letters.

Fill the stocking with candy and small toys, or

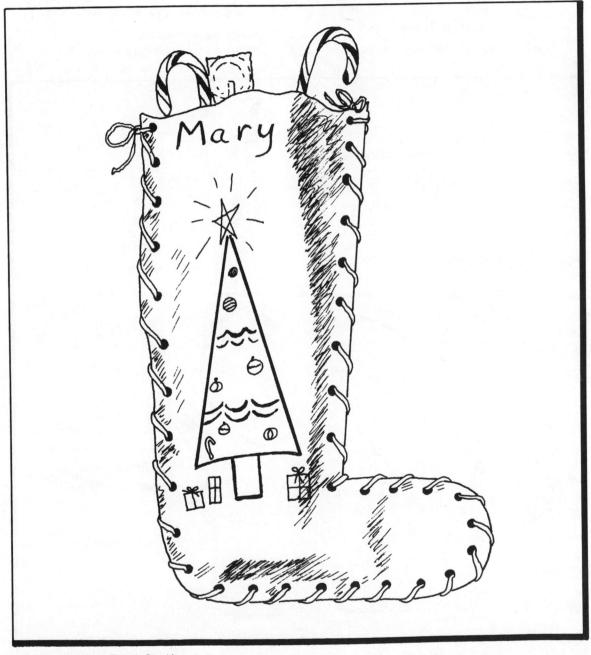

Fig. 12-14. A Paper Punch Stocking.

with a small box of crayons and paper.

## CANDY CANE ELEPHANT

The Candy Cane Elephant makes a delightful tree ornament or holiday decoration (Fig. 12-15).

### Skills to Teach

Teach children 2 years old and up:

- The color *red*
- Gluing skills
- How to use tape
- How to draw a face
- How to tie a knot

Teach children 4 years old and up:

- Tracing and cutting skills
- How to write "Merry Christmas"

Fig. 12-15. The Candy Cane Elephant.

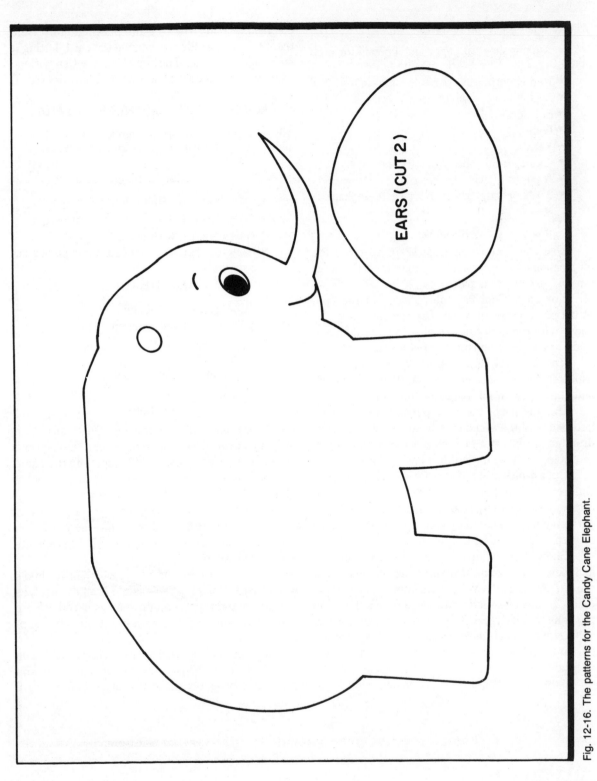

EARS (CUT 2)

Fig. 12-16. The patterns for the Candy Cane Elephant.

### Materials List

- A plain sheet of paper and a pencil for each elephant
- Red construction paper
- A pen
- Scissors
- Glue
- Yarn
- Transparent tape
- A paper punch
- 2 1/2″ candy canes, 1 for each elephant

### Directions

Use the pattern in Fig. 12-16 to trace the elephant and his ears onto the plain paper. Cut them out and use them as patterns.

For each elephant, fold a piece of red construction paper lengthwise. Lay the pattern on the paper with the top of the elephant's back along the fold. Trace the elephant and two ears.

Cut them out, being careful not to cut the fold. Children 4 years old and up can do their own tracing and cutting, with a little help from you.

Use the paper punch to punch a hole through both sides of the elephant's head. Show your children how to insert a 12-inch piece of yarn through this hole, and how to tie it in a knot to form a loop.

Cut a 4-inch piece of yarn for the tail. Help your children tie a knot near one end. They can tape the other end inside the elephant card so most of the yarn sticks out. Then they can separate the strands of yarn on the end of the tail to make a tassle.

Show them where to draw the eyes, mouth, and toes. They can print their names on the front of the elephant, and "Merry Christmas" inside the card. As they draw and write, be sure that they hold the pens correctly. Spell the words out loud to them as they write each letter. Make sure they use uppercase and lowercase letters where they are needed.

Now they can glue one ear on each side of the elephant's head, covering the punched hole. Help them tape the candy cane inside the card, letting it stick out as a trunk. They can hang the Candy Cane Elephant on a door knob or on the Christmas tree.

## NO-COOK PEANUT BUTTER/HONEY BALLS

The final project is a candy that can be made especially for Christmas, or any time for a treat.

### Skills to Teach

Teach children 2 years old and up:

- To sit still, listen, and follow directions
- How to work with dough
- How to write his or her first and last name

### Materials List

- Paper plates and pencils
- A large bowl and wooden spoon
- 1 cup peanut butter
- 1 cup honey
- 2 1/2 cups dry powdered milk

### Directions

Give each child a paper plate. Tell them to turn the plate upside down and to print their first and last names on it. Help each child by spelling the name out loud as he or she writes it. "Your name is spelled M . . . A . . . R . . . Y, Mary."

Help the children measure the peanut butter, honey, and dry powdered milk into the bowl. Let everyone take turns stirring until the ingredients are well blended.

Spoon a portion of dough onto each child's paper plate. The children can eat it all themselves and get a tummy ache, or they can roll it into bite-sized balls to share with the family after supper.

Refrigerate the paper plates with the candy on it for 30 minutes. This candy is even better the next day, but it probably won't last until then.

# Index

# Index

Edited by Suzanne L. Cheatle